FRANCES-JANE FRENCH

THE ABBEY THEATRE SERIES OF PLAYS

A Bibliography

DUFOUR EDITIONS

Set in Times Roman type and printed in the Republic of Ireland
by The Athlone Printing Works for The Dolmen Press Limited
8 Herbert Place, Dublin 2

1970

Distributed outside Ireland, except in the U.S.A. and Canada,
by Oxford University Press
and in the U.S.A. and Canada by
Dufour Editions Inc., Chester Springs, Pa. 19425

CONTENTS

NOTE: Broken Soil, by Padraic Colum was advertised as Vol. IX. of the Series, but was not published in it. The play was subsequently rewritten and published by Maunsel and Company as *The Fiddler's House,* in April, 1907.

LIST OF PLATES

NOTE

The initials in copies examined refer as follows:—F.-J.F. = Frances-Jane French; T.C.D. = Trinity College, Library; N.L.I. = The National Library of Ireland; B.M. = The British Museum; Bod. = The Bodleian Library Oxford; U.C.L. = University Library, Cambridge; A.L.E. = The Advocates' Library, Edinburgh; T.H. = Trinity Hall, Library; R.D.S. = The Royal Dublin Society, Ballsbridge; D.C.L. = Pearse St. Public Library; U.C.D. = University College, Dublin; A.G.I. = Authors' Guild of Ireland; E.McL. = Dr. Edward McLydaght (former Chairman of Maunsel and Co.); R.H.L. = Mr. Lyon (Managing Director of the Talbot Press); L.M. = Mr. Liam Miller; L.S. = Mrs. Lily Stephens; A.B. = Mrs. Thomas Bodkin; D.R. = Mrs. Lennox Robinson; J.O'L. = Mr. John O'Leary; C.P.S. = Mr. Colin Smythe.

N.B.—Under the National Library of Scotland Act, 1925, the Advocates' Library, Edinburgh, was reconstituted as the National Library of Scotland and its copyright privileges were formally transferred to this body.

PREFACE

THIS Bibliography deals with the original *Abbey Theatre Series* of fifteen volumes and the later *Abbey Theatre Series* of nine unnumbered volumes. The front cover of the original series has a line block of Queen Maeve hunting on the Irish hills with an Irish Wolfhound. The line block is from an original woodcut, which was executed circ. 1899, by Elinor Mary Monsell 1878-1953, who was a kinswoman of the first Baron Emly, of Tervoe, Clarina, Co. Limerick. W. B. Yeats admired the original woodcut and it was he who decided to adopt it as the symbol of the new Abbey Theatre on its inception in December, 1904, and it has been used by the theatre as such ever since. The original woodcut is now in the possession of the Abbey Theatre. The later series has a line block of a boy holding a theatrical mask in each hand on the front cover. This line block is also from an original woodcut, but it is unsigned. It has, however, been attributed to Jack Yeats, but this seems to be improbable stylisticly.

The Bibliographical complexity of the books under review has proved extremely tortuous. Quite apart from the difficulty in obtaining access to sufficient copies, I have had to contend with the problem of two, and in one case, three separate publishers using the same sheets for a particular volume. The first three volumes of the original series *(The Well of the Saints; Kincora; The Land)* were first published by the Abbey Theatre itself, and only later republished by Maunsel and Company. The next three volumes, all by W. B. Yeats, were first published by A. H. Bullen in his series, *Plays for an Irish Theatre,* and were then republished by Maunsel and Company. The first volume of the series, by J. M. Synge, was first published by the Abbey Theatre itself, using Bullen's sheets, next by Maunsel and Co. using Bullen's sheets and then by Bullen himself, as Volume IV. of his *Plays for an Irish Theatre.* Matters are further complicated since some of the other volumes in the original series, as well as some of the volumes in the later series, were issued by Maunsel in non-series wrappers. One play, Volume XIV. of the original series, *Birthright* by T. C. Murray, was later issued in the binding of the second series.

The common link between the two series is that all the plays, with the exception of the last play in the later series, *Sable and Gold,* were originally performed by the Abbey Theatre Company or by its predecessor, the Irish Literary Theatre.

Since none of the publishers concerned is any longer in existence, it has been impossible to obtain the number of copies contained in each Edition, Impression or Issue. For the same reason it has not been possible to obtain the exact date of publication or issue. The question of priority of Issues within various Impressions has often been extremely difficult to establish catagorically.

Dating the various Impressions and Issues has been another problem. The *English Catalogue* provides a very rough guide only and is unreliable. The publication dates given by the *English Catalogue* must where possible be verified against Copyright date stamps. Unfortunately, the five Copyright Libraries I have consulted, together with the National Library of Ireland, have not produced very many Copyright Copies. Even the dates on Copyright Copies cannot be relied on without collateral evidence. I have, therefore, had to seek copies in other libraries and in private collections, because of the lack of copies, Copyright or otherwise in Copyright Libraries.

Books bound in wrappers present special Bibliographical problems. The wrappers, unlike any other kind of binding, actually pass through the printing press. So, what would amount to a mere Binding Variant in the case of a book bound in hard covers, becomes in the case of a book bound in wrappers, a genuine Issue arising from the initiative of the Publisher. However, when the printing on the wrappers and the type of paper on which the book is printed, differ from that of the previous Issue, one in fact has a new Impression.

In this present Bibliography, I have found from the *English Catalogue* that several of the volumes were issued intentionally by the publisher in two different bindings on the occasion of their original publication, hence the use of the term " Simultaneous Issue." In such cases, the more expensively bound book is described first.

I am well aware that technically I should have described in full all wording on the wrappers and also all wording of advertisements which are conjugate with the sheets, but for the sake of space, I have merely given sufficient indication of these so as to enable readers to check whether the copies they are inspecting are the same as the ones I have described.

In the Pagination, I have placed the number of pages of advertisements within square brackets, when the advertisements are conjugate with the sheets, but when these are disjunct from the sheets, I have preceded the square brackets by a plus sign.

I have used the term " Description," instead of the more usual term " Contents," as I feel that the word Contents should be reserved for Textual Contents listed at the end of a bibliography of a book.

I think the term " Copies Examined " is preferable to the more conventional term " Location of Copies," since the latter term does not necessarily imply that all copies located were actually individually examined.

I have used Arabic numerals for numbering the volumes, capital letters for the different Impressions, Roman numerals for the different Issues, and lower case letters for Simultaneous Issues. Eg. 17 A Ib = Volume 17, First Impression, First Issue (Simultaneous). I have designed this notation so that it can be readily interpolated should other Issues or Impressions come to light.

All Bibliographies are however incomplete, since it is virtually impossible to examine even one copy of every issue of every impression of every book.   I hope, therefore, that my readers will understand, if they happen to have examined a genuine Issue of a book to which I have not had access.

I am greatly indebted to Professor D. J. Gordon of the University of Reading, who read the original manuscript and who offered much valuable criticism, to Mr. Desmond Harman, who took the photographs for the half-tone blocks, and to the Monotype Corporation Ltd., who supplied the Swash Letters and the Greek type.

INTRODUCTION

BEFORE the inception of the Abbey Theatre in the Winter of 1904-1905, its forerunner, the Irish Literary Theatre, published an occasional magazine *Beltaine* (No. 1, May 1899, No. 2, February 1900, No. 3, April 1900), which was edited by W. B. Yeats. The contents of this magazine were confined to articles concerning the Irish Literary Theatre in general and to lists of its various productions.

In 1901 *Beltaine* was succeeded by *Samhain* which was also edited by W. B. Yeats. The first issue of *Samhain* stated that it was 'Edited for the Irish Literary Theatre,' but the words, 'for the Irish Literary Theatre' were dropped from later issues and the words 'An occasional review' were substituted. *Samhain* was much more ambitious than *Beltaine* and among other things published the texts of a number of plays which were produced by the Irish Literary Theatre or by its successor the Abbey Theatre. No. 1, October 1901—*Casadh an Tsugain* by Douglas Hyde, translated into English as the *Twisting of the Rope* by Lady Gregory, No. 2, October 1902—*Cathleen ni Hoolihan* by W. B. Yeats, and *The Lost Saint* by Lady Gregory, No. 3, September 1903—*Riders to the Sea* by J. M. Synge, and *The Poorhouse* by Douglas Hyde, translated into Irish by Lady Gregory, No. 4, December 1904—*In the Shadow of the Glen* by J. M. Synge, and *The Rising of the Moon* by Lady Gregory, No. 5, November 1905—*Spreading the News* by Lady Gregory, and *An Fear Sinbril* by Lady Gregory, No. 6, December 1906—*Hyacinth Halvey* by Lady Gregory, No. 7, November 1908—*Dervorgilla* by Lady Gregory, and alterations to *Deirdre* by W. B. Yeats).

The Abbey Theatre was founded in December 1904, and in February 1905 the new theatre itself undertook the publishing of certain plays which were produced by the new Company. Hence *The Abbey Theatre Series*. However, plays continued to be published in *Samhain*. The first three volumes of *The Abbey Theatre Series* were originally published by the Abbey Theatre itself.

Sometime in the early Autumn of 1905, Maunsel and Company was founded and the publishing of *The Abbey Theatre Series* was then transferred from the Abbey Theatre to Maunsel and Company. The next three volumes of the series although published *de facto* by Maunsel were in fact totally the work of A. H. Bullen, who supplied the sheets, together with new title pages. The subsequent volumes in the series were published by Maunsel and Company, as well as the last three volumes of *Samhain* (November 1905, December 1906, November 1908), while another number of *Samhain* was planned for 1909, of which only an article by W. B. Yeats seems to have been printed.

It appears, however, that after the founding of Maunsel and Company and the transfer to that firm of *The Abbey Theatre Series* and also the publishing of the periodical *Samhain,* that the Abbey

Theatre in the person of W. B. Yeats still wished to have some organ produced by the Theatre itself. This led to the founding of *The Arrow,* which was published on the following occasions: No. 1, October 20 1906, No. 2, November 24 1906, No. 3, February 23 1907, No. 4, June 1 1907, No. 5, August 25 1909. This periodical, which was also edited by W. B. Yeats, contained notes about the plays produced as well as answers to criticisms about the various plays which the Abbey was then producing. In *The Arrow* (No. 2 November 24 1906) W. B. Yeats, in course of the editorial, wrote, ' we started *The Arrow* very largely that we might reply to hostile criticism of the kind we faced in its abundance last winter.'

Maunsel and Company did more than merely publish the Abbey Theatre plays, they also held the dramatic and other rights of these plays in Ireland and in America. Maunsel and Company also published other Irish plays which were not produced for the first time by the Abbey Theatre or by its predecessor, the Irish Literary Theatre Society. In fact, Maunsel and Company published a total of over seventy plays during the twenty years of their existence between 1905 and 1925. The original *Abbey Theatre Series* ran between 1905 and 1911. After that date, Maunsel and Company continued to publish Abbey Theatre plays intermittently during the next ten years. During this time, they published nine plays which are also called *The Abbey Theatre Series.* These were unnumbered and the line block on the front cover was changed from that designed by Elinor Monsell to one of a boy holding a theatrical mask in each hand. Across the top of this block is the legend Maunsel's and across the bottom is the legend Irish Plays. The block appears never to have been cleaned, with the result that on each successive occasion it was used the design appears more and more blurred.

During the whole of this time Maunsel and Company acted as dramatic agents and published from time to time a catalogue of their Irish Plays, giving the plots, number of characters, etc. Unfortunately, I have not been able to trace any copies of these catalogues, nor have I been able to discover to whom the firm's activities as dramatic agents were transferred, when the firm of Maunsel and Roberts, which Maunsel and Company later became, was closed in 1925.

F.-J. F.

THE ABBEY THEATRE SERIES OF PLAYS

1 A Ia

ABBEY THEATRE SERIES (First Series), Vol. I.
First Impression (First Issue).

John Millington Synge, *The Well of The Saints,* The Abbey Theatre,
Dublin. February, 1905.

THE WELL OF THE SAINTS. | A PLAY IN THREE ACTS. BY | J. M.
SYNGE. | LONDON: A. H. BULLEN. | DUBLIN: THE ABBEY
THEATRE. | 1905.

Printers Imprint: p. *92:* [at foot of page], [hair line] | CHISWICK PRESS:
PRINTED BY CHARLES WHITTINGHAM AND CO. | TOOKS COURT,
CHANCERY LANE, LONDON.

Pagination: pp. *i-iv,* 1-91, *92* = 96 Pages.

Collation Formula: Crown 8vo. [A]² B-F⁸ G⁴ (G₂ + 2G²) = 48 Leaves.

Description: pp. *i-ii* blank; p. *iii* title; p. *iv:* PERSONS. [plus] SCENE.;
pp. 1-91, *92* text; p. *92* Printers Imprint.

Paper: Antique cream laid paper, with deckle foredges.

Binding: Slate grey wrappers, overlapping fore and bottom edges, top edges
opened, other edges untrimmed.

Front Wrapper: Printed black, [line block of Queen Maeve with an Irish
Wolfhound. Size: 10 × 10·8 cms.] | THE WELL OF THE SAINTS, | A
PLAY IN THREE ACTS, BY | J. M. SYNGE. BEING VOL. I. | OF THE
ABBEY THEATRE | SERIES.

Back Wrapper: Printed black, [in right hand bottom corner], [hair line] |
HELY'S, LIMITED, PRINTERS, DUBLIN.

Inside Front Wrapper: [Printed black] *Dramatic and all other rights reserved,
both here and in* | *America.*

Inside Back Wrapper: Printed black, advertisement for The Abbey Theatre
Series, Vol. II.

Format: Crown 8vo.   *Size:* 19·2 × 12·7 cms.

Copies Examined: T.C.D., L.M., L.S., A.B.

Published, February, 1905; Number of Copies: ?500; price, 1/- [Pollard and
MacPhail 18.]

Notes: The sheets of the text are those of the English Edition, published by
A. H. Bullen as Vol. IV. of *Plays for an Irish Theatre* in December, 1905, at
3/6 [Wade 262.]

Bullen printed a special title page for the Dublin Edition. This consists of a
single fold of which p. *i* is tipped in onto the verso of the Front Wrapper, and
p. *iv* is tipped in onto p. *1* of the text. The paper of this tipped in fold is slightly
heavier antique cream laid paper than that of the sheets.

The wrappers were printed in Dublin by Hely's.

Catalogue of Gift Sale at Mansion House, Friday and Saturday, 20 and 21 April, 1935, for The Irish National Aid and Volunteers Dependents Fund, states the number of copies to be 500 Copies and adds a note stating that *The Well of The Saints* is " The rarest of Synge's Works."

L.S.'s copy belonged to Synge. The wrappers are printed in prussian blue. ?Proof Copy. This copy contains slight additions to the text of the second and third acts in Synge's handwriting. These are *not* the revisions incorporated in the *Revised Collected Edition* of the *Plays*, 1932, and to date have not appeared in print.

1 A Ib

?Simultaneous Issue — Sheets of the above Impression in an intentionally different binding.

Binding: Pale green grey, silurian blue boards, ¼ mid bronze green cloth, top edges opened, other edges untrimmed.

Spine: White paper label, printed black, [within a rectangular rule frame, printed green] The | Well | of | the | Saints | J. M. | Synge. | A. H. | BULLEN, | London.

Endpapers: Antique cream laid paper, same as sheets.

Size: 19·3 × 12·8 cms.

Copies Examined: F.-J.F., L.M.

Published, ?February, 1905; price, ?3/6.

Notes: This binding is identical with that used by Bullen for the English Edition of *Plays for an Irish Theatre*, Vol. IV.

P. S. O'Hegarty in *Some Notes on the Bibliography of J. M. Synge, Supplemental to Bourgeois and MacManus* in the *Dublin Magazine*, Vol. XVII., No. I. January-March, 1942, suggested that this Binding Variant was issued by Bullen, in London, at the same time as the book appeared in Dublin, in the Abbey Theatre Series Binding. This certainly seems to be both a plausible and possible explanation.

Not recorded by Pollard and MacPhail.

1 A II

ABBEY THEATRE SERIES (First Series), Vol. I.
First Impression (Second Issue).

John Millington Synge, *The Well of the Saints*, Maunsel and Co. Ltd., Dublin. ? 1905.

THE WELL OF THE SAINTS: | BY J. M. SYNGE | DUBLIN: MAUNSEL AND CO., LTD. | 60, DAWSON STREET. 1905.

Pagination: pp. *i-ii*, 1-91, *92* + [4] = 94 Pages + 4 Pages.

Collation Formula: Crown 8vo.   [A]² (-[A$_{1.2}$] + [A$_2$]) B-F⁸ G⁴ (G$_2$ + 2G²) = 47 Leaves.

Sheets of the First Impression, with a Cancel Title Page.

Binding: Identical with that used for the First Issue.

Front Wrapper: Printed navy blue, [line block of Queen Maeve with an Irish Wolfhound.   Size: 10 × 10·8 cms]. | THE WELL OF THE SAINTS, | A PLAY IN THREE ACTS, BY | J. M. SYNGE, BEING VOL. I. | OF THE ABBEY THEATRE | SERIES.   (Second Edition).

Inside Front Wrapper: Printed navy blue, same as First Issue.

Advertisements: 4 pp. of advertisements, tipped in at end of text, printed on inferior antique cream laid paper, unnumbered, pp. [1-4].   p. [1] fly title: MAUNSEL & CO.'S LIST OF | NEW AND FORTHCOMING BOOKS; p. [2] MAUNSEL & CO.'S NEW BOOKS.; p. [3] ABBEY THEATRE SERIES.; p. [4] [Books] IN PREPARATION.; p. [4] [at foot of page] Hely's Limited, Printers, Dublin.

Format: Crown 8vo.   *Size:* 19·2 × 12·8 cms.

Copies Examined: L.M.

Re-issued,   ?   1905; price, 1/-.

Notes: The sheets of the text are those of the English Edition, published by A. H. Bullen as Vol. IV. of *Plays for an Irish Theatre* in December, 1905, at 3/6 [Wade 262.]

All three Dublin Issues of 1905 lack Yeats' introduction: *Mr. Synge and his Plays*, which is dated: Abbey Theatre, January 27th, 1905.

The title page is a cancel, it consists of a single leaf which is tipped in onto the stub of the original title page.   It is trimmed and is of coarser antique cream laid paper than that of the advertisements, and is an inferior paper to that of the sheets.

Technically, this is a re-issue of the First Impression by a different publisher.

Not recorded by Pollard and MacPhail.

2 A

ABBEY THEATRE SERIES (First Series), Vol. II.
First Impression.

Isabella Augusta Gregory, *Kincora*, The Abbey Theatre, Dublin. ?April, 1905.

KINCORA.   A PLAY IN THREE ACTS. | BY LADY GREGORY. | DUBLIN: THE ABBEY THEATRE, 1905.

Printers Imprint: p. *72:* PRINTED AT THE | [Dublin University Press device] BY PONSONBY & GIBBS.

Pagination: pp. *1-5*, 6, *7*, 8-25, *26*, 27-42, *43*, 44-70, *71-72* = 72 Pages.

Collation Formula: Crown 8vo. [A]² ([A$_1$] + [2A]⁶) B² (B$_1$ + 2B⁶) C² (C$_1$ + 2C⁶) D² (D$_1$ + 2D⁶) E⁴ = 36 Leaves.

Description: p. *1* title; p. *2:* [*Dramatic and all other rights reserved here* | *and in America.*]; p. *3* dedication in facsimile: Abbey Theatre | March 25 – 1905 |

I dedicate this to the | players of tonight | with grateful thoughts of | their endless patience | enthusiasm and courtesy— | Augusta Gregory | [line]; p. *4:* PERSONS.; pp. *5,* 6-70 text; p. *71* date of first production, March, 1905, plus cast, plus note stating that the scenery and costumes were designed by Robert Gregory; p. *72* Printers Imprint.

Paper: Antique cream laid paper.

Binding: Orange brown wrappers, overlapping fore and bottom edges, top edges opened, other edges untrimmed.

Front Wrapper: Printed black, [line block of Queen Maeve with an Irish Wolfhound. Size: 10 × 10·8 cms.] | KINCORA, A PLAY IN THREE | ACTS, BY LADY GREGORY; | BEING VOLUME II. OF THE | ABBEY THEATRE SERIES.

Back Wrapper: Printed black, [bottom right hand corner], [hair line] | HELY's, LIMITED, DUBLIN.

Inside Back Wrapper: Printed black, advertisement for: The Abbey Theatre Series, Vol. I.

Format: Crown 8vo.   *Size:* 19·3 × 12·7 cms.

Copies Examined: T.C.D., N.L.I., B.M., A.B., U.C.D., U.L.C.

Published, ?April, 1905; N.L.I. Stamp, 6 April, 1905; B.M. Stamp, NO 08; U.L.C. Stamp, AU 8 1919; price, 1/-.

Note: Robert Gregory was Lady Gregory's only son, who was killed in action, whilst flying on 23rd January, 1918.

2 B

ABBEY THEATRE SERIES (First Series), Vol. II.
Second Impression.

Isabella Augusta Gregory, *Kincora,* Maunsel and Co., Ltd., Dublin. ? 1906.

KINCORA. | A PLAY IN THREE ACTS. | BY LADY GREGORY. | SECOND EDITION. | DUBLIN: MAUNSEL & CO., LTD., | 60, DAWSON STREET, 1905.

Printed from plates made from the type used for the first impression, with the following alterations: p. *1* title page, reset.

Collation Formula: Same as for the First Impression.

Paper: Same as that used for the First Impression.

Front Wrapper: Printed black, same as that for the First Impression, with the following addition: [after] SERIES. | (Second Edition).

Back Wrapper: Printed black, advertisements for: THE ABBEY THEATRE SERIES [Vol. II. — Vol. VIII.] Other volumes in preparation. [bottom right hand corner], [hair line] | HELY'S LIMITED, DUBLIN.

Inside Back Wrapper: Plain.

Size: 19·5 × 13 cms.

Copies Examined: L.M., U.L.C., A.L.E.

Published, ? 1906; U.C.L. Stamp, FE 14 1908; A.L.E. Stamp, 14 FEB 1908; price, 1/-.

Notes: The *English Catalogue* gives the date of publication as July, 1907. This seems unlikely, as Maunsel and Co. moved their premises from 60, Dawson St. to 96, Middle Abbey St. around April/May, 1906.

The Title Page is *not* a cancel, so this is a new Impression. It is not really a *true* Second Edition, but *only* a Second Impression, being printed from the type used for the First Impression, with the Title Page reset.

Technically, however, this *is* a Second Edition, as it is a new Impression by a different publisher. (N.B. A new Impression published by a different publisher, creates a New Edition).

3 A

ABBEY THEATRE SERIES (First Series), Vol. III.
First Impression.

Padraic Colum, *The Land,* The Abbey Theatre, Dublin. ? 1905.

THE LAND. A PLAY IN THREE ACTS. | BY PADRAIC COLUM. | DUBLIN: THE ABBEY THEATRE, 1905.

Printers Imprint: p. *52* [at foot of page], [hair line] | Printed at the Dublin University Press, by PONSONBY & GIBBS.

Pagination: pp. *i-iv, 1-5,* 6-23, *24,* 25-37, *38,* 39-51, *52* = 56 Pages.

Collation Formula: Crown 8vo. [A]² B² (B₁ + 2B⁶) C² (C₁ + 2C⁶) D² (D₁ + 2D⁶) E² = 28 Leaves.

Description: p. *i* half title: THE LAND.; p. *ii* blank; p. *iii* title; p. *iv:* [*Dramatic and all other rights reserved here* | *and in America.*]; p. *1* dedication: I DEDICATE THIS PLAY TO MY FRIEND | THOMAS KELLY OF NEW YORK.; p. *2* blank; p. *3:* CHARACTERS [plus] Scene; p. *4* blank; pp. *5,* 6-51 text; p. *52* date of first production, June, 1905, plus cast; p. *52* Printers Imprint.

Paper: Antique cream laid paper.

Binding: Pale venetian red wrappers, overlapping fore and bottom edges, top edges opened, other edges untrimmed.

Front Wrapper: Printed deep sepia, [line block of Queen Maeve with an Irish Wolfhound. Size: 10 × 10·8 cms.] | THE LAND, A PLAY IN THREE | ACTS, BY PADRAIC COLUM; | BEING VOLUME III. OF THE | ABBEY THEATRE SERIES.

Inside Back Wrapper: Printed deep sepia, advertisements for: ABBEY THEATRE SERIES. [vols. I. and II.]

Format: Crown 8vo.   *Size:* 19·3 × 12·6 cms·

Copies Examined: L.M., T.C.D., B.M., Bod., U.L.C., A.L.E., A.B.

Published, ? 1905; B.M. Stamp, 28 NO 08; Bod. Stamp, 14.6.1909; U.L.C. Stamp, JU 19 1909; A.L.E. Stamp, 11 JUN 1909; price, 1/-.

Notes: T.C.D.'s copy has 4 pages of Maunsel advertisements, tipped in at end of text, unnumbered, pp. [1-4]. p. [1] fly title: MAUNSEL & CO.'S LIST OF | NEW AND FORTHCOMING BOOKS.; p. [2]: MAUNSEL & CO.'S NEW BOOKS.; p. [3]: ABBEY THEATRE SERIES. [Vols. I. to VII.]; In preparation [Vols. VIII. and IX.]; SAMHAIN.; p. [4] [Books] In Preparation.; p. [4] [at foot of page], [hair line] | Hely's, Limited, Printer's, Dublin.

3 B

ABBEY THEATRE SERIES (First Series), Vol. III.
Second Impression.

Padraic Colum, *The Land,* Maunsel and Co., Ltd., Dublin. ? 1905.

THE LAND. A PLAY IN THREE ACTS. | BY PADRAIC COLUM. | DUBLIN: MAUNSEL & CO., Ltd., | 60 DAWSON STREET, 1905.

Pagination: pp. *i-iv, 1-5, 6-23, 24, 25-37, 38, 39-51, 52* + [4] = 56 Pages + 4 Pages.

Collation Formula: Same as for the First Impression.

Printed from plates made from substantially the same setting o ftype as that used for the First Impression, with the following alterations: p. *iii* title, reset; p. *iv* addition, [in bottom left hand corner] *Second Edition.;* p. 13 addition, eleven lines of text, [after] Ellen. : *Ellen.* May be it is. [and ending] *Matt.* We can, Ellen, we can.; pp. 13-23 type rearranged to allow for the eleven line insertion of new text matter.

Paper: Same as that used for the First Impression.

Binding: Identical with that used for the First Impression.

Front Wrapper: Printed black, same as that of the First Impression, with the following alteration: [fourth line reset] ABBEY THEATRE SERIES [addition] (Second Edition.)

Inside Front Wrapper: Plain.

Advertisements: Same as those in T.C.D.'s First Impression copy.

Size: 19·5 × 13 cms.

Copies Examined: L.M., J.O'L.

Published, ? 1905; price, 1/-.

Notes: The title page is *not* a cancel, so this is a new impression. It is *not* really a (Second Edition), but *only* a Second Impression, which has been revised; being printed from substantially the same setting of type as that used for the First Impression, with the title page reset, and eleven additional lines of text matter on p. 13, and with the tupe on pp. 13-23 rearranged. The Signature on B2 is ? broken and now appears P2.

Technically, however, this *is* a Second Edition, as it is a New Impression by a different publisher.

Hodges Figgis (Booksellers, 6 Dawson St.) had a copy in 1964, with the following pagination: pp. *i-vi, 2/vii, viii, 5, 6-23, 24, 25-37, 38, 39-51, 52* + [4] pp.

advertisements. This copy had brown wrappers and the covers were printed in sepia; size: 19·3 × 12·8 cms. This is probably the copy which D.J.G. now has and bought from H.F. in 1964. The advertisements in D.J.G.'s copy are the same as those in T.C.D.'s First Impression copy and in Second Impression copies. This appears to be a different Impression, on account of the peculiar pagination.

?Proof copy for Second Impression. This copy definitely belongs to a separate binding lot, as the colour of the wrappers, and the colour of the ink in which they are printed differ from those of either the First or Second Impression.

4

ABBEY THEATRE SERIES (First Series), Vol. IV.

William Butler Yeats, *The Hour-Glass, Cathleen Ni Houlihan, The Pot of Broth*, Maunsel and Co., Ltd., Dublin. ? 1905.

THE HOUR-GLASS, CATHLEEN | NI HOULIHAN, THE POT OF | BROTH: BY W. B. YEATS | DUBLIN: MAUNSEL AND CO., LTD. | 60, DAWSON STREET. 1905.

Printers Imprint: p. *84* [Chiswick Press device — a lion rampant leaning on an anchor, around which is entwined a dolphin] | CHISWICK PRESS: CHARLES WHITTINGHAM AND CO. | TOOKS COURT, CHANCERY LANE, LONDON.

Pagination: pp. *i-ii, 1-2,* 3-32, *33-34,* 35-58, *59-60,* 61-82, *83-84* + [4] = 86 Pages + 4 Pages.

Collation Formula: Crown 8vo. [A]¹ B-F⁸ G² = 43 Leaves.

Description: p. *i* title; p. *ii* blank: p. *1* fly title: THE HOUR-GLASS: A MORALITY; p. *2* blank; pp. 3-32 text; p. *33* fly title: CATHLEEN NI HOULIHAN; p. *34* blank; pp. 35-58 text; p. *59* fly title: THE POT OF BROTH; p. *60* blank; pp. 61-82 text; p. *83: NOTE ON THE MUSIC.;* p. *84* Printers Imprint.

Paper: Antique cream laid paper, with deckle foredges.

Binding: Purple wrappers, overlapping fore and bottom edges, top edges opened, other edges untrimmed.

Front Wrapper: Printed black, [line block of Queen Maeve with an Irish Wolfhound. Size: 10 × 10·8 cms.] | THE HOUR GLASS, CATH= | LEEN NI HOULIHAN, THE | POT OF BROTH, BY W. B. | YEATS, BEING VOLUME IV. | OF THE ABBEY THEATRE | SERIES.

Inside Front Wrapper: [Printed black], Dramatic and all other rights reserved | here and in America.

Advertisements: 4 pages of advertisements, printed on antique cream laid paper of slightly inferior quality to that of the sheets, unnumbered, pp. [1-4], tipped in at end of text. P. [1] fly title: MAUNSEL & CO.'S LIST OF | NEW AND FORTHCOMING BOOKS.; p. [2] MAUNSEL & CO.'S NEW BOOKS; p. [3] ABBEY THEATRE SERIES.; p. [4] [Books] IN PREPARATION. [at foot of page], [hair line] | Hely's, Limited, Printers Dublin.

Format: Crown 8vo.   *Size:* 19·1 × 12·8 cms.

Copies Examined: C.P.S., Bod., A.B.

Published,   ?   1905; price, 1/- [Wade 54.]

Notes: There are two lines of music followed by a blank line for music at the top of p. 54; three lines of music at the bottom of p. 55, and four lines of music, beneath one line and one word of type on p. 65.

The sheets of the text are those of the English Edition, [Wade 53,] published by A. H. Bullen as Vol. II. of *Plays for an Irish Theatre* in March, 1904.

Each Quire signed on recto of first leaf with volume number as well as with Signature letter — II. B; II. C; II. D; II. E; II. F; II. G.

Bullen printed a special title page for the Dublin Edition, [Wade 54.] This consists of a single leaf of which p. *i* is tipped in onto the verso of the Front Wrapper, and p. *ii* is tipped in onto p. *1* of the text. The paper of this leaf is of the same antique cream laid paper as the rest of the sheets.

This Edition was for sale in Ireland only and was published by Maunsel and Co. by arrangement with A. H. Bullen (see advertisement in Maunsel Edition of *Ideas of Good and Evil*, [Wade 48].)

Alphonse J. A. Symons in his *Bibliography of First Editions of W. B. Yeats*, 1924, states that "the entire edition comprised 1000 copies." ?The English Edition + The Irish Edition = 1000 copies.

5

ABBEY THEATRE SERIES (First Series), Vol. V.

William Butler Yeats, *The King's Threshold*, Maunsel and Co., Ltd.   ?   1905.

THE KING'S THRESHOLD: | BY W. B. YEATS | DUBLIN: MAUNSEL AND CO., LTD. | 60, DAWSON STREET, 1905.

Pagination: pp. *i-ii*, *1-2*, 3, *4*, 5-9, *10*, 11-66 + [4] = 68 Pages + [4] Pages.

Collation Formula: Crown 8vo.   [A]¹ B-E⁸ F¹ = 34 Leaves.

Description: p. *i* title; p. *ii* blank; p. *1* fly title: THE KING'S THRESHOLD; p. *2* blank; p. *3:* LIST OF CHARACTERS; p. *4* blank; pp. 5-9: PROLOGUE.; p. *10* blank; pp. 11-66 text.

Paper: Antique cream laid paper, with deckle foredges.

Binding: Pale green grey wrappers, overlapping fore and bottom edges, top edges opened, other edges untrimmed.

Front Wrapper: Printed pale grey green, [line block of Queen Maeve with an Irish Wolfhound. Size: 10 × 10·8 cms.] | THE KING'S THRESHOLD, BY | W. B. YEATS, BEING VOL. V. | OF THE ABBEY THEATRE | SERIES.

Inside Front Wrapper: [Printed pale grey green] Dramatic and all other rights reserved | here and in America.

Advertisements: 4 pages of advertisements, printed on antique cream laid paper of slightly lighter quality than that of the sheets, unnumbered, pp. [1-4], tipped in at end of text. p. [1] fly title: MAUNSEL & CO.'S LIST OF | NEW AND FORTHCOMING BOOKS.; p. [2] MAUNSEL & CO.'S NEW BOOKS.; p. [3] ABBEY THEATRE SERIES. [up to Vol. VI.,], [Other vols.] In Preparation.; p. [4] [Books] IN PREPARATION. [at foot of page], [hair line] | Hely's, Limited, Printers, Dublin.

Format: Crown 8vo.   *Size:* 19·1 × 12·4 cms.

Copies Examined: L.M., A.B.

Published,   ?   1905; price, 1/- [Wade 57.]

Notes: The sheets of the text are those of the first part of the English Edition of *Plays for an Irish Theatre*, Vol. III. published by A. H. Bullen in March, 1904, [Wade 56.]

Each Quire signed on recto of first leaf with volume number as well as with Signature letter—III. B; III. C; III. D; III. E; III. F.

Bullen printed a special title page for the Dublin Edition, [Wade] 57. This consists of a single leaf of which p. *i* is tipped in onto the verso of the Front Wrapper and p. *ii* which is tipped in onto p. *1* of the text. The Paper of this tipped in leaf is the same as that of the sheets.

This Edition was for sale in Ireland only and was published by Maunsel and Co. by arrangement with A. H. Bullen (see advertisement in Maunsel Edition of *Ideas of Good and Evil*, [Wade 48].)

Alphonse J. A. Symons in his *Bibliography of First Editions of W. B. Yeats*, 1924, states that " the entire edition comprised 1000 copies." ?The English Edition + The Irish Edition = 1000 copies.

6

ABBEY THEATRE SERIES (First Series), Vol. VI.

William Butler Yeats, *On Baile's Strand*, Maunsel and Co., Ltd., Dublin.   ?December, 1905.

ON BAILE'S STRAND: BY | W. B. YEATS | DUBLIN: MAUNSEL AND CO., LTD. | 60, DAWSON STREET. 1905.

Printers Imprint: p. *118:* [Chiswick Press Device—a lion rampant leaning on an anchor around which is entwined a dolphin] | CHISWICK PRESS: CHARLES WHITTINGHAM AND CO. | TOOKS COURT, CHANCERY LANE, LONDON.

Pagination: pp. *i-ii,* 67-68, 69-117, *118-120* + [4] = 56 Pages + [4] Pages.

Collation Formula: Crown 8vo.   π¹ [F]⁸ (-[F₁]) G-H⁸ I⁴ = 28 Leaves.

Description: p. *i* title; p. *ii* blank; p. *67* fly title: ON BAILE'S STRAND; p. *68* blank; pp. 69-117 text; p. *118* Printers Imprint; pp. *119-120* blank.

Paper: Antique cream laid paper.

*Binding:*Buff wrappers, overlapping fore and bottom edges, top edges opened, other edges untrimmed.

Front Wrapper: Printed orange brown, [line block of Queen Maeve with na Irish Wolfhound. Size: 10 × 10·8 cms.] | ON BAILE'S STRAND, BY W. B. YEATS, BEING VOL. VI. | OF THE ABBEY THEATRE | SERIES.

Inside Front Wrapper: [Printed orange brown] Dramatic and all other rights reserved | here and in America.

Advertisements: 4 pages of advertisements, printed on antique cream laid paper, slightly lighter quality than that of the sheets, with all edges trimmed, tipped in at end of text.

Format: Crown 8vo.   *Size:* 19·3 × 13 cms.

Copies Examined: L.M., N.L.I., A.B.

Published, ?December, 1905; N.L.I. Stamp, 30 DEC 1905; price, 1/- [Wade 58.]

Notes: The advertisements are identical with those in Vol. V.

The Sheets of the text are those of the second part of the English Edition of *Plays for an Irish Theatre,* Vol. III, published by A. H. Bullen in March, 1904, [Wade 56].

Quires, G, H, I, signed on recto of first leaf with volume number as well as with signature letter—III. G; III. H; III. I.

Bullen printed a special title page for the Dublin Edition, [Wade 58.] This consists of a single leaf of which p. *i.* is tipped in onto the verso of the front wrapper, and p. *ii* is tipped in onto p. *67* of the text. The paper of this tipped in leaf is of slightly better quality than that of the sheets and has all its edges trimmed.

This Edition was for sale in Ireland only and was published by Maunsel and Co. by arrangement with A. H. Bullen, (see advertisement in Maunsel Edition of *Ideas of Good and Evil* [Wade 48].)

Alphonse J. A. Symons in his *Bibliography of First Editions of W. B. Yeats,* 1924, states that " the entire edition comprised 1000 cooies." ?English Edition + The Irish Edition = 1000 copies.

7 A

ABBEY THEATRE SERIES (First Series), Vol. VII.
First Impression.

William Boyle, *The Building Fund,* Maunsel and Co., Ltd., Dublin. ? 1905.

THE BUILDING FUND. A PLAY IN | THREE ACTS. BY WILLIAM BOYLE. | DUBLIN: MAUNSEL & CO., LTD., | 60, DAWSON STREET, 1905.

Printers Imprint: None.

Pagination: pp. 1-5, 6-49, 50 + [4] + 50 Pages + 4 Pages.

Collation Formula: Crown 8vo. [A]⁸ B² (B₁ + 2B⁶) C² (C₁ + 2C⁶) D¹ = 25 Leaves.

Description: p. *1* title; p. *2:* [Dramatic and all other rights reserved] p. *3:* PERSONS. [plus] Tᴵᴹᴱ; p. *4* date of first production, 25th April, 1905, plus cast and SCENE; pp. *5,* 6-49 text; p. *50* blank.

Paper: Antique cream laid paper.

22

Binding: Dull grey green wrappers, overlapping fore and bottom edges, top edges opened, other edges untrimmed.

Front Wrapper: Printed very deep sepia, [line block of Queen Maeve with an Irish Wolfhound.   Size: 10 × 10·8 cms.] | THE BUILDING FUND, A | COMEDY IN THREE ACTS, | BY WILLIAM BOYLE, BEING | VOLUME VII. OF THE | ABBEY THEATRE SERIES.

Format: Crown 8vo.   *Size:* 18·8 × 12·5 cms.

Copies Examined: T.C.D., N.L.I., B.M., U.L.C., Bod., A.L.E., A.B.

Published,   ?   1905   T.C.D. Stamp, (on secondary Library binding) Sept. 1909; B.M. Stamp, 18 Jy 07; Bod. Stamp, 14·6·1909; U.L.C. Stamp, JU 15 1909; A.L.E. Stamp, 11 JUN 1909; price, 1/-.

Notes: N.L.I. copy had 4 pages of Maunsel advertisements, printed on inferior antique cream wove paper, tipped in at end of text, unnumbered, pp. [1-4]. p. [1]: MAUNSEL & CO.'S | NEW BOOKS.; p. [2] [new books] NOW READY p. [3] [Books] Ready Immediately; p. [4] blank.

7 B

ABBEY THEATRE SERIES (First Series), Vol. VII.
Second Impression.

William Boyle, *The Building Fund,* Maunsel and Co., Ltd., Dublin. ?   1906.

THE BUILDING FUND. A COMEDY IN | THREE ACTS. BY WILLIAM BOYLE. | SECOND EDITION. | DUBLIN: MAUNSEL & CO., LTD., 1906.

Printers Imprint: p. *50:* DUBLIN: | PRINTED AT THE UNIVERSITY PRESS, | BY PONSONBY AND GIBBS.

Printed from plates made from the type used for the First Impression, with the following alterations: Title page, reset; p. *50* new matter: printers imprint.

Collation Formula: Same as for the First Impression.

Paper: Same as that used for the First Impression.

Binding: Pale olive green wrappers, overlapping fore and bottom edges, top edges opened, other edges untrimmed.

Front Wrapper: Printed black, same as for the First Impression, with the following addition: [after] SERIES | (Second Edition).

Back Wrapper: Printed black, advertisements for: THE ABBEY THEATRE SERIES [Vols. II., III., VIII., IX.] | Other volumes in preparation. | [in right-hand bottom corner], [hair line] | HELY'S, LIMITED, DUBLIN.

Advertisements: 4 pages of Maunsel advertisements, printed on antique cream laid paper, same quality as that of the sheets, tipped in at end of text, numbered, [1], (2-4). p. [1]: NEW AND FORTHCOMING IRISH BOOKS.; The Tower Press Booklets.; p. (2) Advertisements for more new books.; p. (3) Advertisements for: The Northern Leaders of '98.; The Memoirs of Miles Byrne.; NEW BOOK IN IRISH.; p. (4): Works by W. B. Yeats.; ANNOUNCEMENTS.

Size: 19·3 × 12·3 cms.

Copies Examined: L.M., N.L.I.

Issued,   ? 1906; N.L.I. Stamp, 28 Sept. 1908; price, 1/-.

8

ABBEY THEATRE SERIES (First Series), Vol. VIII.

Isabella Augusta Gregory, *The White Cockade*, Maunsel and Co., Ltd., Dublin.   ?1906.

THE WHITE COCKADE. BY LADY | GREGORY. | " *I saw a vision through my sleep last night.*" | *Jacobite Ballad.* | DUBLIN: MAUNSEL & CO., Ltd., | 60, DAWSON STREET, 1905.

Printers Imprint: p. *64:* [hair line] | Printed by Ponsonby & Gibbs, University Press, Dublin.

Pagination: pp. *1-5,* 6-63, *64* + [4] = 64 Pages + 4 Pages.

Collation Formula: Crown 8vo.   [A]⁸ B² (B₁ + 2B⁶) C² (C₁ + 2C⁶) D² (D₁ + 2D⁶) = 32 Leaves.

Description: p. *1* title; p. *2:* [*Dramatic and all other rights reserved here and in* | *America.*]; p. *3* dedication: TO R.G., SCENE-PAINTER.; p. *4:* PERSONS.; pp. *5,* 6-63 text; p. *64* date of first production, December, 1905, plus cast; p. *64* printers imprint.

Paper: Antique cream laid paper.

Binding: Sky blue, silurian grey wrappers, overlapping fore and bottom edges, top edges opened, other edges untrimmed.

Front Wrapper: Printed lavender grey, [line block of Queen Maeve with an Irish Wolfhound.   Size: 10 × 10·8 cms.] | THE WHITE COCKADE, A | COMEDY IN THREE ACTS, | BY LADY GREGORY, BEING | VOLUME VIII. OF THE | ABBEY THEATRE SERIES.

Advertisements: 4 pages of Maunsel Advertisements, printed on antique cream laid paper, same quality as that of the sheets, unnumbered, tipped in at end of text.

Format: Crown 8vo.   *Size:* 19·4 × 12·8 cms.

Copies Examined: L.M., C.P.S., N.L.I., B.M., Bod., U.L.C., A.L.E., A.B.

Published, *English Catalogue,* July, 1907; B.M. Stamp, 19 Jy 07; Bod. Stamp, 16·2·1908; U.L.C. Stamp, FE 14 1908; A.L.E. Stamp, 14 FEB 1908; price 1/-.

Notes: R.G. = Robert Gregory.

The Advertisements are identical with those in Vol. IV. N.L.I. copy is without advertisements.

Although the *English Catalogue* gives the date of publication as July, 1907, and although the B.M. date Stamp bears this out, it is improbable that either is correct, as Maunsel moved their premises from 60, Dawson Street to 96, Middle Abbey Street sometime around April/May, 1906. However, the date 1905 given

on the title page as the date of publication is also improbable, for the four pages
of advertisements tipped in at the end are identical with those in Vol. IV. of
the *Abbey Theatre Series—The Hour Glass, Cathleen ni Houlihan, The Pot of
Broth*, by W. B. Yeats. The N.L.I. date Stamp on Vol. VI.—*On Baile's Strand*
is 30 DEC 1905. Between Vol. VI.—*On Baile's Strand* and Vol. VIII.—*The
White Cockade*, there was Vol. VII.—*The Building Fund*, by William Boyle,
which also has 1905 on the title page and gives Maunsel's address as 60, Dawson
Street. A (Second Edition)—Second Impression of *The Building Fund* was
published in 1906. This Second Impression gives no address for Maunsel and
Co. It advertises *The White Cockade* as being already published, on the back
wrapper. It therefore seems probable that *The White Cockade* was published
sometime between January and April or May, 1906.

9 A

ABBEY THEATRE SERIES (First Series), Vol. IX.
First Impression.

Isabella Augusta Gregory, *Spreading The News, The Rising of
The Moon*. Isabella Augusta Gregory and Douglas Hyde, *The
Poorhouse*, Maunsel and Co. Ltd., Dublin. ?September, 1906.

SPREADING THE NEWS. THE RISING | OF THE MOON. BY LADY
GREGORY. | THE POORHOUSE. BY LADY GREGORY | AND
DOUGLAS HYDE. | DUBLIN: MAUNSEL & CO., Ltd., 1906.

Pagination: pp. *1-5*, 6-29, *30-33*, 34-46, *47-49*, 50-59, *60* + [4] = 60 **Pages**
+ 4 **Pages**.

Collation Formula: Crown 8vo. [A]⁸ B² (B₁ + 2B⁶) C² (C₁ +]⁶) D⁴ E² = 30
Leaves.

Description: p. *1* title; p. *2*: [*Dramatic and all other rights reserved here and in* |
America.]; p. *3* fly title: SPREADING THE NEWS.; p. *4* date of first performance, December 27th, 1904, plus cast; pp. *5*, 6-29 text; p. *30* blank; p. *31*
fly title: THE RISING OF THE MOON.; p. *32*: PERSONS.; pp. *33*, 34-36
text; p. *47* fly title: THE POORHOUSE.; p. *48* Note by Lady Gregory about
writing the play, [signed] Augusta Gregory. | *May* 21, 1906.; pp. *49*, 50-59
text; p. *60* blank.

Paper: Antique cream laid paper.

Binding: Sepia wrappers, overlapping fore and bottom edges, top edges opened,
other edges untrimmed.

Front Wrapper: Printed black, [line block of Queen Maeve with an Irish
Wolfhound. Size: 10 × 10·8 cms.] | SRPEADING THE NEWS, THE |
RISING OF THE MOON, BY | LADY GREGORY: THE POOR- | HOUSE,
BY DOUGLAS HYDE | AND LADY GREGORY; BEING | VOLUME IX.
OF THE ABBEY | THEATRE SERIES.

Back Wrapper: Printed black, advertisement for ABBEY THEATRE SERIES.
[Vols. II., III., VII., VIII.] | Other volumes in preparation. | [bottom right
hand corner], [hair line] | HELY'S, LIMITED, DUBLIN.

Advertisements: 4 pages of Maunsel advertisements, printed on antique cream
laid paper, same quality paper as that of the sheets, numbered, pp. *1* (2-4);
tipped in at end of text. pp. *1* (2-4): NEW & FORTHCOMING IRISH
BOOKS.; p. (4): Works by W. B. Yeats.; ANNOUNCEMENTS.

Format: Crown 8vo.   *Size:* 19·1 × 12·9 cms·

Copies Examined: T.C.D., C.P.S., N.L.I., B.M., A.B.

Published, ?September, 1906; N.L.I. Stamp, 21 SEPT 1906; B.M. Stamp,
19 Jy 07; price, 1/-.

Notes: Douglas Hyde was elected first President of Ireland in 1937.

The Poorhouse was translated into Irish by Lady Gregory and Douglas Hyde
as *TEACH NA mBOCHT*.

Lady Gregory rewrote *The Poorhouse* and first published the revised version
as *The Workhouse Ward* in her *Seven Short Plays* in 1909.

The Poorhouse has not been reprinted since 1907.

9 B

ABBEY THEATRE SERIES (First Series), Vol. IX.
Second Impression.

Isabella Augusta Gregory, *Spreading The News, The Rising of The
Moon.* Isabella Augusta Gregory and Douglas Hyde, *The
Poorhouse,* Maunsel and Co. Ltd., Dublin.   December, 1907.

SPREADING THE NEWS, THE RISING | OF THE MOON. BY LADY
GREGORY. | THE POORHOUSE.   BY LADY GREGORY | AND
DOUGLAS HYDE. | DUBLIN: MAUNSEL & CO., LTD.

Printed from plates made from the type used for the First Impression, with
the following alterations: p. *1* title page, reset; p. *2* addition, [after] *America.* |
Second Edition 1907.

Pagination: pp. *1-5,* 6-29, *30-33,* 34-46, *47-49,* 50-59, *60* + [16] = 60 Pages
+ 16 Pages.

Collation Formula: Crown 8vo. [A]⁸ B² (B₁ + 2B⁶) C² (C₁ + 2C⁶) D⁴ E² = 30
Leaves.

Paper: Same as that used for the First Impression.

Binding: Pale slate purple, silurian grey wrappers, top edges opened, other
edges untrimmed.

Front Wrapper: Printed black, identical to that used for the First Impression.

Back Wrapper: Printed black, advertisements for: Abbey Theatre Series. |
[Vols. II., III., VIII., IX., VII. | [rule] | Library Edition and 25 copies on hand
made paper of THE PLAYBOY OF THE WESTERN | WORLD.

Advertisements: 16 Pages of Maunsel advertisements, printed on antique cream
wove paper, sewn in at end of sheets. Numbered pp. 1-15, *16.* p. 1 [Headed]:
MAUNSEL'S IRISH BOOKS.

Size: 19·3 × 13 cms.

Copies Examined: C.P.S., L.M.

Issued, *English Catalogue,* December, 1907; price, 1/-.

26

10 A

ABBEY THEATRE SERIES (First Series), Vol. X.
First Impression.

John Millington Synge, *The Playboy of The Western World*, Maunsel and Co. Ltd., Dublin.   ?February, 1907.

THE PLAYBOY OF THE | WESTERN WORLD. A |COMEDY IN THREE | ACTS. BY J. M. SYNGE. | THEATRE EDITION | DUBLIN: MAUNSEL | & CO., LTD. 1907.

Printers Imprint: p. *88:* DUBLIN: | PRINTED AT THE UNIVERSITY PRESS, | BY PONSONBY AND GIBBS.

Pagination: pp. *i-iv, 1,* 2-86, *87-88* + [4] — *92* Pages + 4 Pages.

Collation Formula: Crown 8vo.   [A]² B-F⁸ G⁴ = 46 Leaves.

Description: p. *i* title; p. *ii:* [Books] BY THE SAME WRITER. | THE ARAN ISLANDS, with twelve Illustra- | tions by JACK B. YEATS. | THE WELL OF THE SAINTS: a Play in | three Acts. | IN THE SHADOW OF THE GLEN, and | RIDERS TO THE SEA: two Plays.; p. *iii: [Dramatic and all other rights reserved here and in | America.];* p. *iv:* PERSONS. [plus Scene]; pp. *1,* 2-86 text; p. *87* date of first performance, 26th January, 1907, plus cast; p. *88* printers imprint.

Paper: Antique cream laid paper, with deckle foredges.

Binding: Moss green wrappers, overlapping fore and bottom edges, top edges opened, other edges untrimmed.

Front Wrapper: Printed deep green, [line block of Queen Maeve with an Irish Wolfhound.   Size: 10 × 10·8 cms.] | THE PLAYBOY OF THE WEST- | ERN WORLD, A COMEDY IN | THREE ACTS, BY J. M. SYNGE; | BEING VOLUME X. OF THE | ABBEY THEATRE SERIES.

Back Wrapper: Printed deep green, advertisement for: ABBEY THEATRE SERIES. | [Vols. II., III., VIII., IX.] | [heavy rule] | THE PLAYBOY OF THE WESTERN | WORLD, Library Edition, contains a pre- | face and a portrait of the Author, cloth 2/- nett.| ₊*₊ *25 copies on hand-made paper, 5/- nett.*

Advertisements: 4 pages of Maunsel advertisements, printed on antique cream laid paper, of slightly better quality than that of the sheets. Numbered, pp. *1,* (2-4), tipped in at end of text. p. *1* headed: MAUNSEL'S NEW BOOKS.

Format: Crown 8vo.   *Size:* 19·2 × 12·4 cms.

Copies Examined: L.M., T.C.D., B.M., A.B.

Published, ?February, 1907; T.C.D. Stamp, APR 2 1909; B.M. Stamp, 19 Jy 07; price, 1/- [Pollard and MacPhail 28]; [MacManus 5.] note (ii).

Notes: pp. *i-iv* forming a single fold is tipped in, p. *i* onto inside Front Wrapper, and p. *iv* onto p. *1* of the text.

Number altered in MS. on Front Wrapper of T.C.D. copy to XI., but X. is correct, XI. being Thomas MacDonagh's *When the Dawn is Come.*

Technically, this "Theatre Edition" is a Sub-Edition of the "Library Edition" of February, 1907, which contains Synge's preface, and *not* a separate edition.

27

10B

ABBEY THEATRE SERIES (First Series), Vol. X.
Second Impression.

John Millington Synge, *The Playboy of The Western World,*
Maunsel and Co. Ltd., Dublin.   ?November, 1909.

THE PLAYBOY OF THE | WESTERN WORLD. | A COMEDY IN
THREE | ACTS. BY J. M. SYNGE | THEATRE EDITION | MAUNSEL
& CO., LTD., | 96 MID. ABBEY ST., DUBLIN.

Printers Imprint: p. *88:* DUBLIN: | PRINTED AT THE UNIVERSITY
PRESS, | BY PONSONBY AND GIBBS.

Pagination: pp. *i-v,* vi-vii, *viii, 1,* 2-86, *87-88* = 96 Pages.

Collation Formula: Crown 8vo. [A]⁴ B-F⁸ G⁴ = 48 Leaves.

Description: p. *i* half title: THE PLAYBOY OF THE WESTERN WORLD;
p. *ii* [Books] BY THE SAME WRITER. | THE ARAN ISLANDS. Illustrated
by | JACK B. YEATS. THE WELL OF THE SAINTS. | IN THE SHADOW
OF THE GLEN. | RIDERS TO THE SEA. | THE TINKER'S WEDDING.;
p. *iii* title; p. *iv:* First Printed, . . . February, 1907. | Reprinted, ... April, 1907. |
[ditto marks] . . . . *June, 1909.* | [*Performing and all other rights reserved here
and in* | *America.*]; pp. *v,* vi-vii: PREFACE. [signed] J.M.S. | *January 21st,
1907.;* p. *viii:* PERSONS. [plus Scene]; pp. *1,* 2-86 text; p. *87* date of first
performance, 26th January, 1907, plus cast; p. *88* printers imprint.

Paper: Antique cream laid paper, with deckle foredges.

Binding: Grey green wrappers, overlapping fore and bottom edges, top edges
opened, other edges untrimmed.

Front Wrapper: Printed grey green, [line block of Queen Maeve with an Irish
Wolfhound. Size: 10 × 10·8 cms.] | The Playboy of the West=| ern World, a
Comedy in | Three Acts, by J. M. Synge; | being Volume X. of the | Abbey
Theatre Series.

Back Wrapper: Printed grey green, advertisements for : IRISH PLAYS.

Format: Crown 8vo.   *Size:* 19·2 × 13 cms.

Copies Examined: L.M.

Reissue, *English Catalogue,* November, 1909; price, 1/-.

Notes: The Front Wrapper has been reset.

Technically, this is a hybrid Impression, conforming to neither the " Library
Edition " conditions, nor to the " Theatre Edition " conditions.

The date of publication given in the *English Catalogue* is quite likely to be
correct. For, although the prelims. and the text are identical with the " Library
Edition," Third Impression of June, 1909, the title page has been reset, with
the deliberate inclusion of the words: THEATRE EDITION.

Not recorded by Pollard and MacPhail.

28

11

ABBEY THEATRE SERIES (First Series), Vol. XI.

Thomas MacDonagh, *When The Dawn Is Come*, Maunsel and Co. Ltd., Dublin. February, 1908.

WHEN THE DAWN IS COME | A TRAGEDY IN THREE ACTS | BY THOMAS MacDONAGH | DUBLIN: MAUNSEL | & COMPANY, LTD. 1908.

Printers Imprint: p. 48 [at foot of page] Printed by JOHN FALCONER, 53 Upper Sackville Street, Dublin.

Pagination: pp. *1-7*, 8-18, *19*, 20-42, *43*, 44-48 = 48 Pages.

Collation Formula: Crown 8vo. [A]⁸ B-C⁸ = 24 Leaves.

Description: p. *1* half title: WHEN THE DAWN IS COME; p. *2* [within a hair-line panel frame] BOOKS OF VERSE | BY THOMAS MacDONAGH | [hair line] | " THROUGH THE IVORY GATE " | (SEALY, BRYERS & WALKER) | " THE GOLDEN JOY " | (O'DONAGHUE & Co.); p. *3* title; p. *4: Dramatic and all other rights reserved;* p. *5* dedication: *To M.;* p. *6:* PERSONS [plus Scene]; pp. *7*, 8-48 text; p. 48 at foot of page, Printers Imprint.

Paper: Antique cream wove paper.

Binding: Ochre, silurian grey wrappers, overlapping fore and bottom edges, top edges opened, other edges untrimmed.

Front Cover: Printed sepia, [line block of Queen Maeve with an Irish Wolf-hound. Size: 10 × 10·8 cms.] WHEN THE DAWN IS | COME. A TRAGEDY IN | THREE ACTS. BY | THOMAS MacDONAGH; | BEING VOLUME X. (sic) OF | THE ABBEY THEATRE | SERIES.

Format: Crown 8vo.   *Size:* 19·3 × 12·3 cms.

Copies Examined: L.M., N.L.I., B.M., Bod., U.L.C., A.L.E., A.B.

Published, *English Catalogue*, February, 1908; N.L.I. Stamp, 23 OCT 1908; B.M. Stamp, 28 NO 08; Bod. Stamp, 14.11.1908; U.L.C. Stamp, 11 NOV 1908; A.L.E. Stamp, 11 NOV 1908; price, 1/-.

Notes: X. on the Front Cover is a misprint for XI. In later binding lots, the " I " is inserted, sometimes in ink and sometimes by a rubber stamp.

Thomas MacDonagh was one of the leaders of the 1916 Rebellion and one of the signatories of the 1916 Proclamation. He was subsequently executed for the prominent part he played in the Rising.

12

ABBEY THEATRE SERIES (First Series), Vol. XII.

Esmé Stuart Lennox Robinson, *The Cross Roads*, Maunsel and Co. Ltd., Dublin. November, 1909.

THE CROSS-ROADS. A | PLAY IN A PROLOGUE | AND TWO ACTS. BY | S. L. ROBINSON | MAUNSEL AND CO., LIMITED | 96, MID. ABBEY ST., DUBLIN.

Pagination: pp. *1-5*, 6-59, *60*, [4] = 64 Pages.

Collation Formula: Crown 8vo. [A]⁸ B² (B₁ + 2B⁶) C²(C₁ + 2C⁶) D²(D₁ + 2D⁶) = 32 Leaves.

Description: p. *1* half title: THE CROSS-ROADS; p. *2* blank; p. *3* title; p. *4:* *Performing and all other rights reserved. Per- | mission to perform this play must be obtained from* | MAUNSEL & CO. LTD. *96 Middle Abbey Street,* | *Dublin.;* pp. *5*, 6-59 text; p. *60* date of first production, 1st April, 1909, plus cast.

Paper: Antique cream wove paper.

Binding: Mid orange brown wrappers, overlapping fore and bottom edges, top edges opened, other edges untrimmed.

Front Wrapper: Printed red brown, [line block of Queen Maeve with an Irish Wolfhound. Size: 10 × 10·8 cms.] | THE CROSS ROADS. A PLAY | BY S. L. ROBINSON: BEING | VOL. XII. OF THE ABBEY | THEATRE SERIES.

Back Wrapper: Printed red brown, advertisements for : IRISH PLAYS.

Advertisements: 4 Pages of advertisements conjugate with the last gathering of the sheets, unnumbered, pp. [1-4]. p. [1]: MAUNSEL'S IRISH PLAYS. | A Special List of Plays available for performance, | with fees, and full par- | ticulars of number of char- | acters in each play, a synopsis of the plots, also | the time required for performance, can be had on | application.; p. [2] [Books] By LADY GREGORY.; By W. B. YEATS; By J. M. SYNGE.; p. 3 [Books] By PADRAIC COLUM.; By RUTHERFORD MAYNE.; By WILLIAM BOYLE.; By LEWIS PURCELL.; By SEUMAS O'KELLY.; By THOMAS MACDONAGH.; p. [4]: NEW AND FORTHCOMING | PUBLICATIONS.

Format: Crown 8vo.   *Size:* 19 × 12·8 cms.

Copies Examined: F.-J.F. (2 copies), L.M., N.L.I., B.M., Bod., A.B.

Published, *English Catalogue,* November, 1909; N.L.I. Stamp, 25 Nov. 1909; B.M. Stamp, 12 FE 10; Bod. Stamp, 31·8·1910; price, 1/-.

13 A I

ABBEY THEATRE SERIES (First Series), Vol. XIII.
First Impression (First Issue).

Padraic Colum, *Thomas Muskerry*, Maunsel and Co. Ltd., Dublin, May, 1910.

THOMAS MUSKERRY A | PLAY IN THREE ACTS | BY PÁDRAIC COLUM | DUBLIN: MAUNSEL & CO., LTD | 1910.

Pagination: pp. *1-3*, 4-5, *6-7*, 8-30, *31*, 32-47, *48*, 49-64 = 64 Pages.

Collation Formula: Crown 8vo. [A]⁸ B-D⁸ = 32 Leaves.

Description: p. *1* title; p. *2: Permission to perform this play in Ireland and Great Britain | must be obtained from Maunsel & Co., Ltd., | 96 Middle Abbey Street, Dublin;* pp. *3*, 4-5 dedication in the form of a letter: To T.H.K. [starting] MY DEAR FRIEND, [signed] PADRAIC COLUM, | *April,* 1910.; p. *6:* CHARACTERS: pp. *7*, 8-64 text, p. 64 date of first production, 5th May, 1910, plus cast.

Paper: Antique cream wove paper.

Binding: Sepia wrappers, overlapping fore and bottom edges, top edges opened, other edges untrimmed.

Front Wrapper: Printed very deep bottle green, [line block of Queen Maeve with an Irish Wofhound.   Size: 10 × 10·8 cms.] | THOMAS MUSKERRY. A | PLAY IN THREE ACTS.   BY | PADRAIC COLUM; BEING | VOLUME XIII. OF THE | ABBEY THEATRE SERIES.

Back Wrapper: Printed very deep bottle green, [within a hair line frame] A List of Irish Plays giving | Plots, Number of Characters, &c., | and Particulars of Acting Fee can | be had on application to— | MAUNSEL & CO., Ltd.

Format: Crown 8vo.   *Size:* 19·2 × 13·2 cms.

Copies Examined: F.-J.F., T.C.D., B.M., Bod., U.L.C., A.L.E., A.B.

Published, *English Catalogue*, May, 1910; T.C.D. Stamp, 6 MAY 1910; B.M. Stamp, 6 SE 10; Bod. Stamp, 8·5·1911; U.L.C. Stamp, My 1 1911; A.L.E. Stamp, 1 MAY 1911; price, 1/-.

13 A II

ABBEY THEATRE SERIES (First Series), Vol. XIII.
First Impression (Second Issue).

Padraic Colum, *Thomas Muskerry,* Maunsel and Co. Ltd., Dublin, October, 1911.

Sheets of the First Impression bound in an intentionally different binding.

Binding: Sepia boards, all edges trimmed.

Front Cover: Printed black, [across upper portion] THOMAS MUSKERRY | A PLAY IN THREE ACTS, | [in centre], [small line block of Queen Maeve with an Irish Wolfhound.   Size: 5 × 5·5 cms.] | [beneath] BY PADRAIC COLUM.

Spine: Printed black, [horizontally along spine, near head, reading upwards] THOMAS MUSKERRY.

Endpapers: Coarser antique wove paper than that of the sheets.

Advertisements: 4 pages of Maunsel advertisements, tipped in at end of text, on slightly thinner antique cream wove paper than that of the sheets, unnumbered, pp. [1-4].   p. [1] *Just Published.;* THE CASE FOR HOME RULE.; p. [2] HOME RULE FINANCE.; p. [3] IRELAND AND THE HOME RULE MOVEMENT.; LABOUR IN IRISH HISTORY.; p. [4] THE UNITED IRISH WOMEN,; NOBLESSE OBLIGE.; CLERICAL INFLUENCES.

Size: 18·4 × 12·3 cms.

Copies Examined: F.-J.F., A.B.

Issued, *English Catalogue*, October, 1911; price, 1/6.

Notes: If the date of publication given by the *English Catalogue* is correct, then *this* volume does constitute a genuine Second Issue, for in addition to the advertisements, some of which *do* advertise books which were published in 1911; the binding is a deliberate order from the Publishers for a new style, and is not merely a fortuitous event originating with the binder.

F.-J.F.'s copy is without the advertisements.

14 A I

ABBEY THEATRE SERIES (First Series), Vol. XIV.
First Impression (First Issue).

Thomas Cornelius Murray, *Birthright,* Maunsel and Co. Ltd., Dublin, April, 1911.

BIRTHRIGHT | A PLAY IN TWO ACTS | BY T. C. MURRAY | MAUNSEL AND CO., LTD., | 96 MID. ABBEY ST., DUBLIN. | 1911.

Pagination: pp. *1-5*, 6-43, *44*, [4] = 48 Pages.

Collation Formula: Crown 8vo. [A]⁸ B-C⁸ = 24 Leaves.

Description: p. *1* title; p. *2:* Copyright 1911.   *T. C. Murray.* | *All rights reserved.* | *Permission to perform this Play must be obtained from the Publishers.;* p. *3* [dedication]: TO YOU WHOSE CHARACTER | SUGGESTED THAT OF MAURA | MORRISSEY IN THIS PLAY I | LOVINGLY DEDICATE THIS | LITTLE VOLUME. | T. C. M.; p. *4:* PERSONS IN THE PLAY.; pp. *5*, 6-43 text; p. *44* date of first production, 27th October, 1910, plus cast.

Paper: Antique cream wove paper.

Binding: Pale blue grey wrappers, overlapping fore and bottom edges, top edges trimmed, other edges untrimmed.

Front Wrapper: Printed dark blue, [line block of Queen Maeve with an Irish Wolfhound.   Size: 10 × 10·8 cms.] | BIRTHRIGHT: A PLAY | IN TWO ACTS, BY T. C. | MURRAY, BEING VOL. | XIV. OF THE ABBEY | THEATRE SERIES.

Back Wrapper: Printed dark blue, advertisements for: SOME IRISH PLAYS.

Inside Front Wrapper: Printed dark blue, note about Maunsel's Catalogue.

Inside Back Wrapper: Printed dark blue, advertisements for Books by Lady Gregory.

Advertisements: 4 pages of advertisements conjugate with the last gathering of the sheets, unnumbered, pp. [1-4].   p. [1]: RECENT PUBLICATIONS; pp. [2-3] Books by J. M. Synge; p. [4] Books by Lady Gregory and by Ella Young.

Format: Crown 8vo.   *Size:* 18·9 × 12·8 cms.

Copies Examined: T.H., L.M., F.-J.F., N.L.I., B.M., Bod., A.L.E., J.O'L., A.B.

Published, *English Catalogue,* April, 1911; N.L.I. Stamp, 25 APR. 1911; B.M. Stamp, 2 SEP 11; Bod. Stamp, 3.2.1912; A.L.E. Stamp, 31 JAN 1912; price, 1/-.

Notes: Birthright was translated into Irish by Máire ní Shíothcháin as OIDHREACHT.

PLATE 1   Birthright, Vol. XIV. (Abbey Theatre Series — First Series)
First Impression, First Issue (bound in first series wrappers)

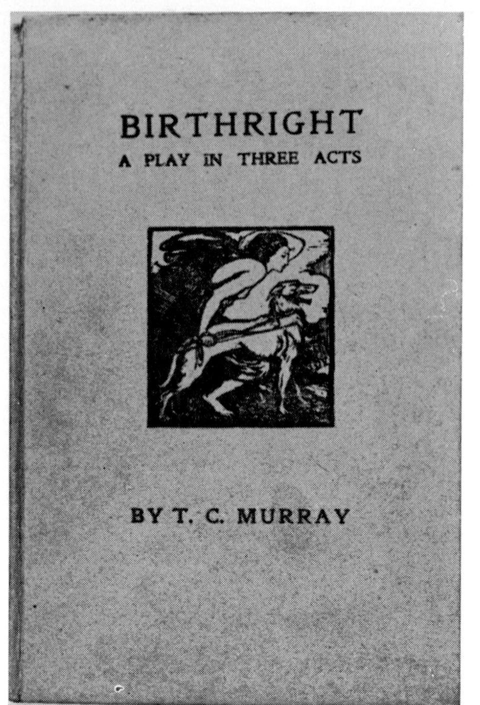

a.

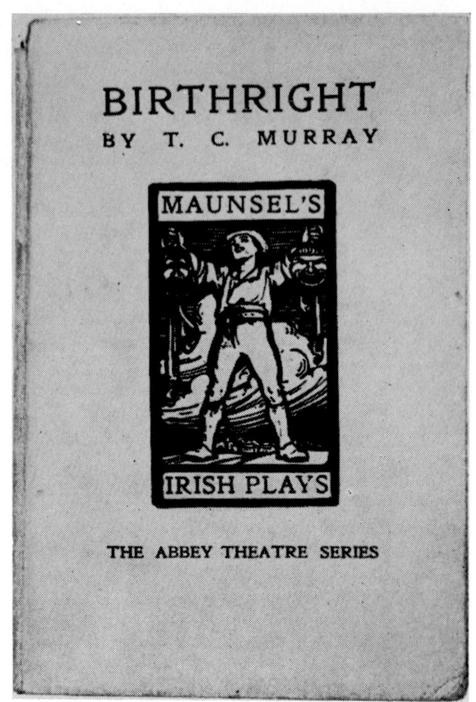

b.

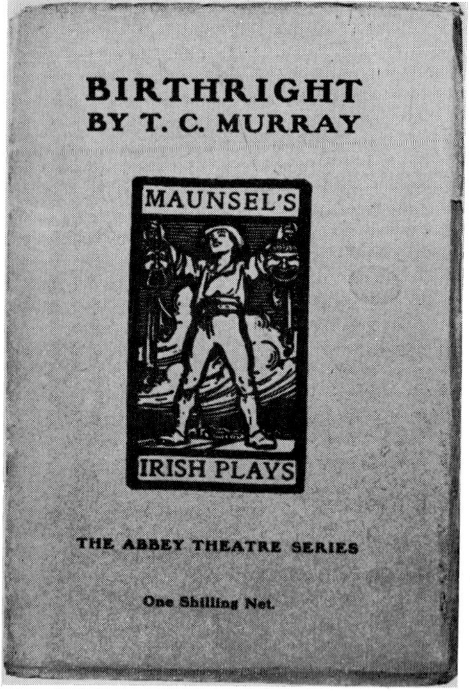

c.

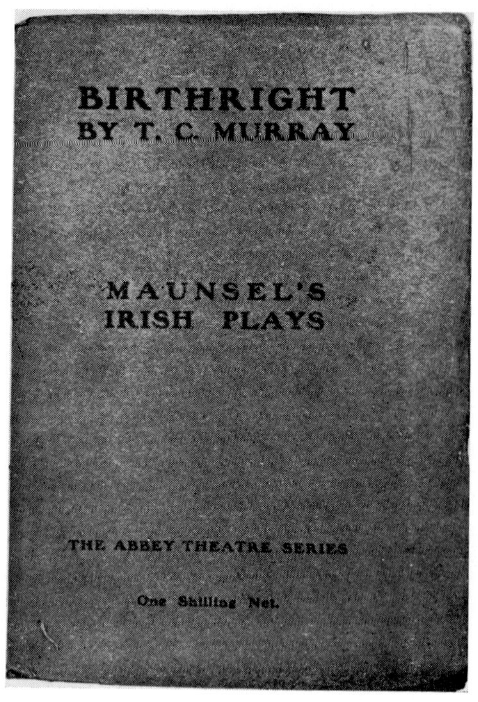

d.

PLATE 1I   Birthright, Vol XIV (Abbey Theatre Series — First Series)
    a. First Impression, Second Issue (bound in first series boards)
    b. Second Impression (bound in second series boards)
    c. Third Impression, First Issue (bound in second series wrappers)
    d. Third Impression, Second Issue (bound in out of series wrappers)

14 A II

ABBEY THEATRE SERIES (First Series), Vol. XIV.
First Impression (Second Issue).

Thomas Cornelius Murray, *Birthright*, Maunsel and Co. Ltd.,
Dublin, ?October, 1911.

Sheets of the First Impression bound in an intentionally different binding.

Binding: Pale blue grey silurian prussian blue boards, all edges trimmed.

Front Cover: Printed dark blue, [across upper portion] BIRTHRIGHT | A
PLAY IN THREE ACTS | [in centre], [small line block of Queen Maeve with
an Irish Wolfhound. Size: 5 × 5·5 cms.] | [beneath] T. C. MURRAY.

Spine: Printed dark blue, [horizontally along spine, near head, reading upwards]
BIRTHRIGHT.

Endpapers: Antique cream laid paper.

Size: 18·5 × 12 cms.

Copies Examined: F.-J.F.

Issued, *English Catalogue*, October, 1911.

Notes: The date given here by the *English Catalogue*, is the same as that given
by the *English Catalogue* for the Second Issue of *Thomas Muskerry*, so it is
possible that the Second Issue of each was in fact issued in October, 1911.

14 B

ABBEY THEATRE SERIES (First Series), Vol. XIV.
Second Impression.

Thomas Cornelius Murray, *Birthright*, Maunsel and Co. Ltd.,
Dublin, ? 1912.

BIRTHRIGHT | A PLAY IN TWO ACTS | BY T. C. MURRAY |
MAUNSEL AND CO., LTD., | 96 MID. ABBEY ST., DUBLIN.

Pagination: pp. *1-5*, 6-43, *44* + [4] = 44 Pages + 4 Pages.

Collation Formula: Crown 8vo. [A]⁸ B⁸ C⁶ = 22 Leaves.

Printed from plates made from the type used for the First Impression, with
the following alterations: p. *1* title page, ommission: 1911; p. *2* addition, in
centre of page: *First Printed 1911 | Reprinted 1912.*

Paper: Same as that used for the First Impression.

Binding: Identical to that used for the First Impression, Second Issue.

Front Cover: Printed deep blue, [across upper portion] BIRTHRIGHT | BY
T. C. MURRAY | [line block of a boy holding a theatrical mask in each hand.
Size: 9 × 5 cms. Across top of block: MAUNSEL'S [and] across bottom of
block: IRISH PLAYS | [beneath] THE ABBEY THEATRE SERIES.

Spine: Printed deep blue, [horizontally along spine, near head, reading upwards] BIRTHRIGHT.

Endpapers: Inferior antique cream wove paper.

Advertisements: Original advertisements, which were conjugate with the sheets, omitted. Instead, 4 pages of new advertisements tipped in at end of text, printed on the same paper as that of the sheets, unnumbered, pp. [1-4]. pp. [1-2] Books by J. M. Synge; p. [3] Books by Lady Gregory and by Rutherford Mayne; p. [4] Plays by Lady Gregory; by George Moore; by Lennox Robinson and by St. John Ervine.

Size: 18·5 × 11·9 cms.

Copies Examined: L.M.

Issued,   ?   1912; price, 1/6.

14 C I

ABBEY THEATRE SERIES (First Series), Vol. XIV.
Third Impression (First Issue).

Thomas Cornelius Murray, *Birthright,* Maunsel and Co. Ltd., Dublin,   ?

BIRTHRIGHT | A PLAY IN TWO ACTS | BY T. C. MURRAY | MAUNSEL AND CO., LTD., | 96 MID. ABBEY ST., DUBLIN.

Pagination: 1-5, 6-43, 44, = 44 Pages.

Collation Formula: Same as for Second Impression.

Printed from plates made from the type used for the First Impression, including the alterations made in the Second Impression, with the following alterations from the Second Impression: p. *2* omission: *First Printed 1911* | *Reprinted 1912.*

Paper: Same as that used for the First and Second Impressions.

Binding: Green grey wrappers, overlapping all edges, all edges trimmed.

Front Wrapper: Printed black, reset, [across upper portion] BIRTHRIGHT | BY T. C. MURRAY | [line block of a boy holding a theatrical mask in each hand]. Size: 9 × 5 cms. Across top of block: MAUNSEL'S [and] across base of block: IRISH PLAYS | [beneath] THE ABBEY THEATRE SERIES | One Shilling Net.

No advertisements.

Size: 18·8 × 12·6 cms.

Copies Examined: L.M., J. O'L.

Issued,   ?   ; price, 1/-.

14 C II

ABBEY THEATRE SERIES (First Series), Vol. XIV.—
Third Impression (Second Issue).

Thomas Cornelius Murray, *Birthright*, Maunsel and Co. Ltd.,
Dublin.   ?

Sheets of the Third Impression, bound in the following binding:

Binding: Slate prussian blue wrappers, overlapping all edges, top edges trimmed,
other edges untrimmed.

Front Wrapper: Printed black, [across upper portion] BIRTHRIGHT | BY
T. C. MURRAY | [across centre] MAUNSEL'S | IRISH PLAYS | [across
lower portion] THE ABBEY THEATRE SERIES | One Shilling Net.

Size: 18·8 × 12·6 cms.

Copies Examined: A.G.I.

Issued,   ?   ; price, 1/-.

15

ABBEY THEATRE SERIES (First Series), Vol. XV.

St. John Greer Ervine, *Mixed Marriage*, Maunsel and Co. Ltd.,
Dublin. June, 1911.

MIXED MARRIAGE: | A PLAY IN FOUR ACTS | BY ST. JOHN G.
ERVINE | MAUNSEL & COMPANY, LTD. | 96 MID. ABBEY STREET,
DUBLIN | 1911.

Pagination: pp. *i-iv, 1,* 2-12, *13,* 14-24, *25,* 26-45, *46,* 47-55, 56 + [4] = 60
Pages + 4 Pages.

Collation Formula: π² A-B⁸ [C]⁸ [D]⁴ = 30 Leaves.

Description: p. *i* title; p. *ii:* Copyright 1911. St. John G. Ervine | All Rights
Reserved; p. *iii* dedication: *To* | *NORA*; p. *iv:* PERSONS IN THE PLAY;
pp. *1,* 2-55 text; p. *56* date of first production, 30th March, 1911, plus cast.

Paper: Antique cream wove paper.

Binding: Sage green wrappers, overlapping all edges, top edges trimmed, other
edges untrimmed.

Front Wrapper: Printed dark grey green, [line block of Queen Maeve with an
Irish Wolfhound. Size: 10 × 10·8 cms.] | MIXED MARRIAGE: | A PLAY
IN FOUR ACTS, | By ST. JOHN G. ERVINE, | BEING VOL. XV. OF |
THE ABBEY THEATRE | SERIES.

Back Wrapper: Printed dark grey green, advertisements for: SOME IRISH
PLAYS.

Inside Front Wrapper: Printed dark grey green, advertisement for Maunsel's
Catalogue of Books by Irish Writers and Books about Ireland.

Inside Back Wrapper: Printed dark grey green, advertisement for: SEVEN SHORT PLAYS. By Lady Gregory.

Advertisements: Four pages of Maunsel advertisements, tipped in at end of text, printed on antique cream wove paper, same quality as that of the sheets, unnumbered, pp. [1-4]. p. 1: RECENT PUBLICATIONS; pp. [2-3] Books by J. M. Synge; p. 4 Books by T. M. Kettle; by L. Paul Dubois and by James Connolly.

Format: Crown 8vo.   *Size:* 18·6 × 12·6 cms.

Copies Examined: F.-J.F., L.M., T.C.D., N.L.I., B.M., Bod., U.L.C., A.L.E., J.O'L., A.B.

Published, *English Catalogue*, June, 1911; T.C.D. Stamp, 6 Sept 1911; N.L.I. Stamp, 27 NOV 1912; B.M. Stamp, 2 SEP 11; Bod. Stamp, 3·2·1912; U.L.C. Stamp, 29 JA 1912; A.L.E. Stamp, 31 JAN 1912; price, 1/-.

Notes: The Title page consists of a single fold of p. *1* is tipped in onto the inside Front Wrapper and p. *iv* is tipped in onto p. *1* of the text.

The advertisements are identical with those in Vol. XIV.—First Impression, except that pp. [1] and [4] are transposed here.

L.M.'s copy has on Back Wrapper, advertisements for: J. M. SYNGE'S BOOKS.

The *English Catalogue* also states that *Mixed Marriage* was published in boards at 1/6 in June, 1911. I have so far failed to locate such a copy, although I have been informed by several people that such does in fact exist.

Mixed Marriage was subsequently published (Second Edition) by George Allen and Unwin, in 1920. B.M. Stamp, 26 JAN 21.

16

ABBEY THEATRE SERIES (Second Series), Vol. 1.

Isabella Augusta Gregory, *The Image*, October, 1911.

THE IMAGE A PLAY | IN THREE ACTS BY | LADY GREGORY | DUBLIN: MAUNSEL & CO., LTD | 96 MIDDLE ABBEY STREET | 1910.

Pagination: pp. *i-vi*, 1-98, *99*, 100-102, *103-104* = 110 Pages.

Collation Formula: Crown 8vo. π⁴(-π₁) A-F⁸ G⁶ = 55 Leaves.

Description: p. *i* title; p. *ii: Copyright 1910, Lady Gregory | All rights reserved;* p. *iii* dedication: TO MY NEPHEWS HUGH | LANE AND JOHN SHAWE- | TAYLOR, IMAGE-MAKERS; pp. *iv-vi* blank; pp. 1-98 text; pp. *99,* 100-102: NOTES; pp. *103-104* blank.

Paper: Antique cream wove paper.

Binding: Slate grey boards, all edges trimmed.

Front Cover: Printed black, [across upper portion] THE IMAGE | BY LADY GREGORY | [line block of a boy holding a theatrical mask in each hand], across top of block: MAUNSEL'S [and] across base of block: IRISH PLAYS. Size: 9 × 5 cms.] | [beneath] THE ABBEY THEATRE SERIES.

Spine: Printed black, [horizontally along spine, near head, reading upwards]
THE IMAGE.

Endpapers: Thin antique cream wove paper.

Format: Crown 8vo.   *Size:* 18·3 × 11·9 cms.

Copies Examined: E.McL.

Published, *English Catalogue*, October, 1911; price, 1/6.

Notes: The Image was originally published in 1910, *English Catalogue*, June,
1910. The *English Catalogue* describes the book as being sewn—sewn implies
wrappers. There was in fact an earlier impression of the book with wrappers
published in 1910. N.L.I. has a copy, with the date stamp, 15 JUN 1910. This
copy is printed on antique cream laid paper. The *English Catalogue* describes
the October, 1911, impression as having boards. A Second Impression *was*
printed sometime between June, 1910, and October, 1911. This Second Impression is printed on antique cream wove paper, and the full stop is omitted after
" LTD " on the title page. This impression is found in two different bindings:

1. *Wrappers*—similar to the First Impression of June, 1910, the price having
been reduced to 1/- from 1/6. The back wrapper carries an advertisement for
RECENT PLAYS, including *Birthright*, by T. C. Murray, which was published
in October, 1911. It is therefore fair to conclude that this Second Impression
was put on sale around the same time.

2. *Boards*—this is the book described above. So, I take it that some sheets of
the Second Impression were bound in the *Abbey Theatre Series* binding, thus
creating a Second Issue, and put on sale also in October, 1911, the date recorded
in the *English Catalogue*.

D.R. has a copy which is possibly a ?Binding Sample for the October, 1911,
Second Impression issue in Boards. It Collates as follows: π^4 A-F^8 G^4 = 56
Leaves, π_1 being blank. The Front Cover is printed black, [across upper por-
tion] THE IMAGE | BY LADY GREGORY The spine is missing. *Size:*
18·5 × 11·11 cms.

17 A Ia

ABBEY THEATRE SERIES (Second Series), Vol. 2.
First Impression (First Issue).

Esmé Stuart Lennox Robinson, *Patriots*, Maunsel and Co. Ltd.,
Dublin. June, 1912.

PATRIOTS | A PLAY IN THREE ACTS | BY LENNOX ROBINSON |
MAUNSEL & COMPANY, Ltd. | DUBLIN AND LONDON | 1912.

Printers Imprint: p. [6]: Dublin: Printed by John Falconer.

Pagination: pp. *i-viii, 1,* 2-49, *50-52* + [6] = 60 Pages + 6 Pages.

Collation Formula: Crown 8vo. π^4 A-C^8 [D]^2 = 30 Leaves.

Description: p. *i* half title: PATRIOTS; p. *ii* blank; p. *iii* title; p. *iv: Copyright*
1912. *Lennox Robinson* | All rights reserved.; p. *v* Theme: *Costello.* It's a
statue of Liberty Brian Hosty was talking | about in the commencement |
Mannion. Ah, who the hell cares about liberty? . . . | THE IMAGE (*Lady Gregory*).;

p. *vi* blank; p. *vii* Acts and page numbers; p. *viii:* CHARACTERS.; pp. *1,* 2-49 text; p. *50* blank; p. *51* date of first production, April 11th, 1912, plus cast; p. *52* blank.

Paper: Antique cream wove paper.

Binding: Grey boards, all edges trimmed.

Front Cover: Printed black, [across upper portion] PATRIOTS | BY LENNOX ROBINSON | [line block of a boy holding a theatrical mask in each hand, across top of block: MAUNSEL'S [and] across base of block: IRISH PLAYS.

Size: 8·9 × 5 cms. | [beneath] THE ABBEY THEATRE SERIES.

Spine: Printed black, [horizontally along spine, near head, reading upwards] PATRIOTS.

Endpapers: Antique cream wove paper of slightly inferior quality to that of the sheets.

Advertisements: Four pages of Maunsel advertisements, printed on antique cream wove paper, same quality as that of the sheets, unnumbered, pp. [1-4] tipped in at end of text. p. [1] Plays by Lennox Robinson; by St. John G. Ervine and by Rutherford Mayne; p. [2] Plays by Lady Gregory; by George Moore and by T. C. Murray; p. [3]: BOOKS ABOUT IRELAND; p. [4]: Recent Publications.

Format: Crown 8vo.   *Size:* 18·4 × 12·8 cms.

Copies Examined: F.-J.F., T.C.D., B.M., Bod., A.L.E.

Published, *English Catalogue,* June, 1912; T.C.D. Stamp, 5 JAN 1912, ?(misprint for JUN); B.M. Stamp, 17 JUN 12; Bod. Stamp, 30.7.1912; A.L.E. Stamp, 26 JUL 1912; price, 1/6.

Notes: B.M., Bodleian and A.E.L. Copies have grey olive green boards.

Between p. [4] of the advertisements and the back endpaper, there is a single leaf tipped in, printed on the same antique cream wove paper as the sheets. Recto of this leaf is blank, Verso—Printers Imprint.

L.M. has a copy which lacks the tipped in leaf with the Printers Imprint at the end of the book.

17 A Ib

?Simultaneous Issue—Sheets of the First Impression issued in an intentionally different binding.

Binding: Dark yellow green wrappers, overlapping all edges, all edges trimmed.

Front Wrapper: Printed black, [within a wide rule frame with mitred corners] [across upper portion] PATRIOTS | BY LENNOX ROBINSON | [across lower portion] MAUNSEL & CO., LIMITED | ONE SHILLING NET.

Back Wrapper: Printed black, advertisements for: J. M. SYNGE'S BOOKS.

Inside Front Wrapper: Printed black, advertisements for books by Lady Gregory.

Inside Back Wrapper: Printed black advertisement for: SEVEN SHORT PLAYS. By Lady Gregory.

Size: 19·3 × 13 cms.

Copies Examined: D.R., N.L.I., Bod.

Published, *English Catalogue*, June, 1912; N.L.I. Stamp, 26 NOV 1912; price, 1/-.
price, 1/-.

Notes: The *English Catalogue* describes the book as being sewn—sewn implies
wrappers. So, I think it is fair to assume that this is the book referred to in the
English Catalogue as being published in June, 1912, at 1/-.

There is no tipped in leaf between the advertisements and the inside Back
Wrapper.

The Bodleian copy has top edges opened, other edges untrimmed. The advertisements inside the Front Wrapper and inside the Back Wrapper are transposed,
?Another Issue.

17 A II

?Later Issue: Similar to the First Issue in Wrappers, but with a tipped in leaf
between pp. *iv* and *v*. Recto of leaf dedication: TO THE JAMES NUGENTS
OF HISTORY; Verso of leaf, blank.
Collation Formula: π^4 ($\pi_2 + \chi^1$) A-C^8 [D]^2 = 31 Leaves.

Front Wrapper: Printed black, partly reset, lower part now reads: MAUNSEL
AND COMPANY LTD. | DUBLIN AND LONDON | One Shilling net.

Advertisements on inside Front Wrapper and on inside Back Wrapper are
transposed as in the Bodleian copy.

Size: 18·6 × 12·3 cms.

Copies Examined: F.-J.F., A.G.I.

Notes: J.O'L. has a copy with binding and advertisements on Wrappers similar
to F.J.F.'s and A.G.I.'s copies, but lacking the tipped in leaf between pp. *iv*
and *v*. Collation Formula, same as for the First Issue.

17 B

J.O'L. has a copy with the same grey olive green boards as B.M. and Bod.
copies, and without the tipped in leaf at the end of the book, with the Printers
Imprint. This copy collates as follows: π^6 ($-\pi_6$) A-C^8 [D]^2 = 31 Leaves.

?Different Impression. For between pp. iv and v there is an extra leaf conjugate
with the sheets, recto [dedication]: TO | THE JAMES NUGENTS | OF
HISTORY; verso: blank. Size: 18·4 × 11·9 cms. This copy has the same four
pages of advertisements tipped in at the end of text as have the other copies in
boards.

18 A I a

ABBEY THEATRE SERIES (Second Series), Vol. 3.

Joseph Campbell, *Judgment*, Maunsel and Co. Ltd., Dublin. June, 1912.

JUDGMENT | A PLAY IN TWO ACTS | BY JOSEPH CAMPBELL | MAUNSEL & CO., LTD. | DUBLIN AND LONDON | 1912.

Pagination: pp. *i-viii, 1,* 2-35, *36* + [4] = 44 Pages + 4 Pages.

Collation Formula: π⁴ A-B⁸ C² = 22 Leaves.

Description: p. *i* half title: JUDGMENT; p. *ii* [within a light rule panel frame] BY THE SAME AUTHOR | The Mountainy Singer. Poems. | Mearing Stones. Notes in Don- | gal :: illustrated by the Author; p. *iii* title; p. *iv:* Copyright 1912, Joseph Campbell | All rights reserved; p. *v* dedication: *TO* | *N. C.;* p. *vi* blank; p. *vii:* PREFACE [signed] J. C.; p. *viii:* CHARACTERS [plus] Scene; pp. *1,* 2-35 text; p. *36* Place and date of first production, 15th April, 1912.

Paper: Antique cream wove paper.

Binding: Venetian red boards, all edges trimmed.

Front Cover: Printed black, [across upper portion] JUDGMENT | BY JOSEPH CAMPBELL | [line block of a boy holding a theatrical mask in each hand, across top of block: MAUNSEL'S [and] across base of block: IRISH PLAYS. Size: 9 × 5 cms.] | [beneath] THE ABBEY THEATRE SERIES.

Advertisements: Four pages of Maunsel advertisements, printed on same antique cream wove paper as sheets, unnumbered, pp. [1-4], tipped in at end of text. p. [1] Books by Joseph Campbell; by Seosamh MacCathmhaoil; p. [2] Plays by Lennox Robinson; by St. John G. Ervine and by Rutherford Mayne; p. [3] Plays by Lady Gregory; by George Moore and by T. C. Murray; p. [4]: Recent Publications.

Spine: Printed black, [horizontally along spine, near head, reading upwards] JUDGMENT.

Endpapers: Lighter quality antique cream wove paper than that of the sheets.

Format: Crown 8vo.   *Size:* 18·4 × 12·2 cms.

Copies Examined: T.H., T.C.D., B.M., Bod., A.L.E., U.L.C., J.O'L.

Published, *English Catalogue,* June, 1912; T.C.D. Stamp, 15 Jan 1912 (pubr). ?Misprint for JUN; B.M. Stamp, 17 JUN 12; Bod. Stamp, 16·10·1912; U.L.C. Stamp, 14 OCT 1912; A.L.E. Stamp, 14 OCT 1912; price, 1/6.

Notes: N.C. = Nancy Campbell—Joseph Campbell's wife.

Seosamh MacCathmhaoil is the Irish version of Joseph Campbell's name.

18 A I b

Simultaneous Issue: Sheets of the First Impression issued in an intentionally different binding.

Binding: Orange brown wrappers, overlapping all edges, all edges trimmed.

Front Wrapper: Printed black, [within a wide rule frame with mitred corners], [across upper portion] JUDGMENT | BY JOSEPH CAMPBELL | (Seosaṁ maccaṫṁaoil) | [across lower portion] MAUNSEL & CO., LIMITED | ONE SHILLING NET.

Back Wrapper: Printed black, advertisements for: J. M. SYNGE'S BOOKS.

Inside Front Wrapper: Printed black, advertisement for: SEVEN SHORT PLAYS. By Lady Gregory.

Inside Back Wrapper: Printed black, advertisements for books by Lady Gregory.

Size: 18·5 × 12·3 cms.

Copies Examined: F.-J.F.

Published, *English Catalogue*, June, 1912; price, 1/-.

19 A Ia

ABBEY THEATRE SERIES (Second Series), Vol. 4.
First Impression (First Issue).

Thomas Cornelius Murray, *Maurice Harte*, Maunsel and Co. Ltd., Dublin. June, 1912.

MAURICE HARTE | A PLAY IN TWO ACTS | BY T. C. MURRAY | MAUNSEL AND CO., LTD., | DUBLIN AND LONDON | 1912.

Pagination: pp. *1-5*, 6-60, *61*, [3] = 64 Pages.

Collation Formula: Crown 8vo. [A]⁸ B-⁸C D⁶ E⁴ = 32 Leaves.

Description: p. *1* title; p. *2: Copyright 1912. T. C. Murray. | All rights reserved. |*

Permission to perform this Play must be obtained from | the Publishers.; p. *3* dedication: TO MY WIFE AND MY LITTLE BOY AND GIRL, MY | PLAY'S FIRST AUDIENCE; p. *4: PERSONS IN THE PLAY* [plus] Scene; pp. *5*, 6-60 text; p. *61* date and place of first performance: Royal Court Theatre, London, in June, 1912, by the Abbey Theatre Company, [plus] cast.

Paper: Antique cream wove paper.

Binding: Blue grey boards, all edges trimmed.

Front Cover: Printed prussian blue, [across upper portion] MAURICE HARTE | BY T. C. MURRAY | [line block of a boy holding a theatrical mask in each hand, across top of block: MAUNSEL'S [and] across base of block: IRISH PLAYS. Size: 9 × 5·1 cms. | [beneath] THE ABBEY THEATRE SERIES.

Spine: Printed prussian blue, [horizontally along spine, near head, reading upwards] MAURICE HARTE.

Endpapers: Antique cream wove paper, same as sheets.

Advertisements: Three pages of Maunsel advertisements, conjugate with the sheets, forming the last three pages of a tipped in single fold, of which the first page is p. *61*. Advertisements unnumbered, pp. [1-3]. P. [1] Plays by T. C.

Murray; by Lady Gregory and by George Moore; p. [2] Plays by Lennox
Robinson; by St. John G. Ervine and by Rutherford Mayne; p. [3]: Recent
Publications.

Format: Crown 8vo.   *Size:* 18·4 × 12 cms.

Copies Examined: B.M., Bod., U.L.C., A.L.E.

Published, *English Catalogue,* June 1912; B.M. Stamp, 15 JUL 12, Bod. Stamp,
16.10.1912; U.L.C. Stamp, 14 OC 1912; A.L.E. Stamp, 14 OCT 1914; price, 1/6.

Notes: Maurice Harte was translated into Irish by Tomás Ó Gallċobaiṗ as
Muiris Ó hAiṗt.

19 A Ib

Simultaneous Issue: Sheets of the First Impression issued in an intentionally
different binding.

Binding: Grey sage green wrappers, overlapping all edges, top edges trimmed,
other edges untrimmed.

Front Wrapper: Printed black, [across upper portion] MAURICE HARTE |
BY T. C. MURRAY | [line block of a boy holding a theatrical mask in each
hand, across top of block: MAUNSEL S [and] across base of block: IRISH
PLAYS. Size: 6 × 5·1 cms.] | [beneath] THE ABBEY THEATRE SERIES |

One Shilling Net.

Size: 19 × 12·9 cms.

Copies Examined: T.H.

Published, *English Catalogue,* June, 1912; price, 1/-.

19 A II

ABBEY THEATRE SERIES (Second Series), Vol. 4
First Impression (Second Issue).

Thomas Cornelius Murray, *Maurice Harte,* Maunsel and Co.
Ltd., Dublin.   ?November, 1912.

Sheets of the First Impression, bound in an intentionally different binding.

Binding: Blue grey, silurian prussian blue wrappers, overlapping all edges, all
edges trimmed.

Front Wrapper: Printed navy blue, [within a wide rule frame, with mitred
corners], [across upper portion] MAURICE HARTE | BY T. C. MURRAY |
[across lower portion] MAUNSEL & COMPANY LTD. | DUBLIN AND
LONDON | One Shilling net.

Spine: Printed navy blue, [horizontally along spine, near head, reading upwards]
MAURICE HARTE.

42

Back Wrapper: Printed navy blue, advertisements for: J. M. SYNGE'S BOOKS.

Inside Front Wrapper: Printed navy blue, advertisements for books by Lady Gregory.

Inside Back Wrapper: Printed navy blue, advertisement for: SEVEN SHORT PLAYS. By Lady Gregory.

Size: 19 × 12·8 cms.

Copies Examined: F.-J.F., N.L.I.

Issued, ?November, 1912; N.L.I. Stamp, 27 NOV 1912; price, 1/-.

20 A Ia

ABBEY THEATRE SERIES (Second Series), Vol. 5.

Seamus O'Kelly, *The Bribe*, February, 1914.

THE BRIBE | A PLAY IN THREE ACTS | BY SEUMAS O'KELLY | *Author of " The Shuiler's Child," " The Matchmakers,"* &c. | MAUNSEL & COMPANY, LTD. | DUBLIN AND LONDON | 1914.

Special Imprint: p. *48* [at foot of page] *Printed in Dublin for Maunsel & Co.*

Pagination: pp. *i-iv, 1*, 2-46, *47-48* = 52 Pages.

Collation Formula: Crown 8vo.   π² A-C⁸ = 26 Leaves.

Description: p. *i* title; p. *ii* [at foot of page] Copyright, 1914, Seumas O'Kelly; p. *iii:* CHARACTERS [plus] SCENE; p. *iv* blank; pp. *1*, 2-46 text; p. *47* date of first performance, 18th December, 1913, plus cast; p. *48* Special Imprint.

Paper: Antique cream wove paper.

Binding: Green grey silurian bottle green boards, all edges trimmed.

Front Cover: Printed bottle green, [across upper portion] THE BRIBE | BY SEUMAS O'KELLY | [line block of a boy holding a theatrical mask in each hand, across top of block: MAUNSEL'S [and] across base of block: IRISH PLAYS.   Size: 9 × 5·1 cms.] | [beneath] THE ABBEY THEATRE SERIES.

Spine: Printed bottle green, [horizontally along spine, near head, reading upwards] THE BRIBE.

Endpapers: Antique cream wove paper, same quality as the sheets.

Format: Crown 8vo.   *Size:* 18·4 × 12·1 cms.

Copies Examined: B.M.

Published, *English Catalogue*, February, 1914; B.M. Stamp, 9 APR 14; price, 1/6.

20 A Ib

Simultaneous Issue: Sheets of the First Impression, issued in an intentionally different binding.

Binding: Green grey, silurian bottle green wrappers, overlapping all edges, all edges trimmed.

Front Wrapper: Printed black, [within a wide rule frame, with mitred corners] [across upper portion] THE BRIBE | BY SEUMAS O'KELLY | [across lower portion] MAUNSEL AND COMPANY LTD. | DUBLIN AND LONDON | One Shilling net.

Back Wrapper: Printed black, advertisement for: J. M. SYNGE'S BOOKS.

Inside Front Wrapper: Printed black, note about Maunsel's Catalogue.

Inside Back Wrapper: Printed black, advertisement for: SEVEN SHORT PLAYS. By Lady Gregory.

Size: 18.2 × 12.1 cms.

Copies Examined: F.-J.F., T.C.D., Bod., A.L.E., A.G.I., R.D.S.

Published, *English Catalogue*, February, 1914; T.C.D. Stamp, 15 APR 1914; Bod. Stamp, 17.6.1914; A.L.E. Stamp, 16 JUN 1914; R.D.S. Stamp, 19 MAR 1914; price, 1/-.

21 A Ia

ABBEY THEATRE SERIES (Second Series), Vol. 6.
First Impression (First Issue).

George Fitzmaurice, *The Country Dressmaker*, Maunsel and Co. Ltd., Dublin. April, 1914.

THE COUNTRY | DRESSMAKER | A PLAY IN THREE ACTS | BY GEORGE FITZMAURICE | MAUNSEL & COMPANY, LTD. | DUBLIN AND LONDON · 1914.

Printers Imprint: p. *2* [at foot of page] *Printed by* R. & R. CLARK, LIMITED, *Edinburgh.*

Pagination: pp. *1-2*, 3-57 *58-60*, = 60 Pages.

Collation Formula: Crown 8vo. [B]⁸ C-D⁸ E⁶ = 30 Leaves.

Description: p. *1* title; p. *2:* COPYRIGHT 1914. GEORGE FITZMAURICE | CHARACTERS [plus] Scene | [Printers Imprint]; pp. 3-57 text; pp. *58-60* blank.

Paper: Antique cream laid paper.

Binding: Pale green, silurian grey boards, all edges trimmed.

Front Cover: Printed deep blue green, [across upper portion] THE COUNTRY DRESSMAKER | BY GEORGE FITZMAURICE. | [line block of a boy holding a theatrical mask in each hand, across top of block: MAUNSEL'S [and] across base of block: IRISH PLAYS. Size: 9·9 × 5 cms. | [beneath] THE ABBEY THEATRE SERIES.

Spine: Printed deep blue green, [horizontally along spine, near head, reading upwards] THE COUNTRY DRESSMAKER.

Endpapers: Antique cream laid paper, same quality as sheets.

44

Format: Crown 8vo.   *Size:* 18·3 × 12·5 cms.

Copies Examined: R.H.L., B.M.

Published, *English Catalogue*, April, 1914; B.M. Stamp, 9 APR 14; price, 1/6.

21 A Ib

Simultaneous Issue: Sheets of the First Impression, bound in an intentionally different Binding.

Binding: Pale green grey wrappers, overlapping all edges, all edges trimmed.

Front Wrapper: Printed deep blue green, [within a wide rule frame, with mitred corners], [across upper portion] THE COUNTRY DRESSMAKER | BY GEORGE FITZMAURICE | [across lower portion] MAUNSEL & COMPANY LTD. | DUBLIN AND LONDON | One Shilling net.

Back Wrapper: Printed deep blue green, advertisements for: J. M. SYNGE'S BOOKS.

Inside Front Wrapper: Printed deep blue green, note about Maunsel's Catalogue.

Inside Back Wrapper: Printed deep blue green, advertisement for: SEVEN SHORT PLAYS. By Lady Gregory.

Size: 18·4 × 12·6 cms.

Copies Examined: F.-J.F., T.C.D., Bod.

Published, *English Catalogue,* April, 1914; T.C.D. Stamp, 15 APR 1914; Bod. Stamp, 17·6·1914; A.L.E. Stamp, 16 JUN 1914; price, 1/-.

*Notes:*1,000 copies were printed, but I have been unable to discover how they were split between the two Issues.

21 B I

ABBEY THEATRE SERIES (Second Series), Vol. 6.
Second Impression (First Issue).

George Fitzmaurice, *The Country Dressmaker,* Maunsel and Roberts, Ltd., Dublin.? ?1921.

THE COUNTRY | DRESSMAKER | A PLAY IN THREE ACTS | BY GEORGE FITZMAURICE | MAUNSEL AND ROBERTS LTD. | DUBLIN AND LONDON. 1921.

Printer's Imprint: p. *57* [at foot of page] Printed by George Roberts, Dublin. Printed from plates made from the type used for the First Impression, with the following alterations: p. *1* title page, partly reset; p. *2* printers imprint omitted; p. *57* new printers imprint; pp. *59-60* removed.

Pagination: pp. *1-2, 3-57, 58* = 58 Pages.

[*Collation Formula:* Crown 8vo. [B]⁸ C-D⁸ E⁸ (-E₈) = 29 Leaves.

Paper: Antique cream wove paper.

Binding: Mid bronze green wrappers, all edges trimmed.

Front Wrapper: Printed black, [within a wide rule frame, with mitred corners], [across upper portion] THE COUNTRY | DRESSMAKER | BY GEORGE FITZMAURICE | [across lower portion] MAUNSEL & ROBERTS LTD. | DUBLIN AND LONDON | One Shilling Net.

Back Wrapper: Printed black, advertisements for books by Padraic Pearse and by John M. Synge.

Inside Front Wrapper: Printed black, advertisements for books about Ireland.

Inside Back Wrapper: Printed black, advertisements for books about Ireland; IRISH NOVELS.

Size: 18·6 × 12·1 cms.

Copies Examined: A.G.I., D.C.L., U.C.D.

Issued,   ?   1921; price, 1/-.

21 B II

Sheets of the Second Impression bound in a Talbot Press Binding.

Binding: Dove grey, silurian slate grey wrappers, all edges trimmed.

Front Wrapper: Printed bottle green, [in fancy letters, across upper portion] THE TALBOT | PRESS PLAYS | [line block of two theatrical masks, one touching and the other overlapping a wide and a narrow rule] | [a fancy rule] | [in scarlet] *THE COUNTRY* | *DRESSMAKER* | *GEORGE FITZMAURICE* [in bottle green], [a fancy rule] | [narrow rule] | [wide rule] | [in outline letters] TALBOT PRESS LTD. | [in script] Dublin and Cork.

Size: 18·1 × 12·2 cms.

Copies Examined: U.C.D.

Issued,   ?   Price, ?

Notes: The Talbot Press bought the sheets of a number of Maunsel's books at Maunsel and Roberts' auction in April, 1926, and bound these sheets in their own bindings.

22 A

ABBEY THEATRE SERIES (Second Series), Vol. 7.
First Impression.

Edward McNulty, *The Lord Mayor*, Maunsel and Co. Ltd., Dublin. June 1917.

THE LORD MAYOR | A DUBLIN COMEDY IN THREE ACTS | BY EDWARD McNULTY | *As played at the Abbey Theatre* | MAUNSEL AND

CO., LTD. | 50 LR. BAGGOT STREET, DUBLIN | 40 MUSEUM STREET, LONDON | 1917.

Printers Imprint: p. *52* [at foot of page] Printed by George Roberts, Dublin.

Pagination: pp. *i-iv*, 1-50, *51-52* = 56 Pages.

Collation Formula: Crown 8vo. [A]² B-D⁴ E³ = 28 Leaves.

Description: p. *i* title; p. *ii:* Copyright 1917. Edward McNulty; p. *iii: Permission to perform this play | must be obtained from the Pub- | lishers. Fees for amateur per- | formances in halls, One Guinea | for each performance, payable | before the performance, takes place. | Performances in Theatres, and in | Dublin, Belfast, and Cork, by | special arrangement only.;* p. *iv: CHARACTERS* [plus] *TIME;* pp. 1-50 text; p. *51* blank; p. *52* Printers Imprint.

Paper: Antique cream wove paper.

Binding: Sage green wrappers, overlapping all edges, all edges trimmed.

Front Wrapper: Printed black, [across upper portion] THE LORD MAYOR | A DUBLIN COMEDY | BY EDWARD McNULTY | [line block of a boy holding a theatrical mask in each hand, across top of block: MAUNSEL'S [and] across base of block: IRISH PLAYS. Size: 8·9 × 5 cms.] | [beneath] ABBEY THEATRE SERIES | One Shilling Net.

Format: Crown 8vo.   *Size:* 18·7 × 12·1 cms.

Copies Examined: F.-J.F., T.C.D., N.L.I., B.M., Bod., A.L.E., J.O'L.

Published, *English Catalogue*, June, 1917; T.C.D. Stamp, 25 SEPT 1917; N.L.I. Stamp, 7 JUN 1917; B.M. Stamp, 28 SEP 17; Bod. Stamp, 4 JUL 1918; A.L.E. Stamp, 26 JUN 1918; price, 1/-.

22 B

ABBEY THEATRE SERIES (Second Series), Vol. 7.
Second Impression.

Edward McNulty, *The Lord Mayor*, Maunsel and Co. Ltd., Dublin. ?September, 1919.

Printed from plates made from the type used for the First Impression.

Paper: Very inferior wartime buff coloured newsprint.

Binding: Light blue wrappers, overlapping all edges, all edges trimmed.

Front Wrapper: Printed black, identical with Front Wrapper of First Impression.

Size: 18·5 × 12·2 cms.

Copies Examined: A.G.I. (2 copies).

Issued, ?September, 1919; price, 1/-.

Notes: In ink across right hand top corner of Front Wrapper of one of A.G.I.'s copies: M. ff. Mackeown B.A. | Sept. 19.

C 22

ABBEY THEATRE SERIES (Second Series), Vol. 7.
Third Impression.

Edward McNulty, *The Lord Mayor*, Maunsel and Roberts, Ltd., Dublin.   ?

THE LORD MAYOR | A DUBLIN COMEDY IN THREE ACTS | BY EDWARD McNULTY | *As played at the Abbey Theatre* | MAUNSEL & ROBERTS, LTD. | 50 LR. BAGGOT STREET, DUBLIN.

Printed from plates made from the type used for the previous Impressions, with the following alterations: p. *1* title page, lower part reset.

Paper: Very inferior buff wove paper (newsprint).

Binding: Deep drab brown, silurian pale drab brown wrappers, all edges trimmed.

Front Wrapper: Printed black, identical with front wrappers of previous Impressions.

Inside Front Wrapper: Printed black, [in centre] *TO AMATEURS* | *All communications should be addressed* | *To the Author, 71 Strand Road, Sandy-* | *mount, Dublin. Fee per Performance:* | *One Guinea.*

Size: 18·3 × 12·1 cms.

Copies Examined: L.M.

Issued,   ?   ; price, 1/-.

Notes: The date of issue must be between the dates 1920 and 1925, for the firm of Maunsel and Co. became Maunsel and Roberts in 1920, and was closed in 1925.

L.M.'s copy has the last leaf, E_2, roughly torn out, so it is impossible to tell whether the Printers Imprint has been altered.

23

ABBEY THEATRE SERIES (Second Series), Vol. 8.

John Bernard McCarthy, *Crusaders*, Maunsel and Co. Ltd., Dublin. July, 1918.

CRUSADERS | A PLAY IN TWO ACTS | BY J. BERNARD McCARTHY | MAUNSEL & COMPANY, LTD. | DUBLIN AND LONDON. 1918.
Printers Imprint: p. *ii* [at foot of page] Printed by George Roberts, Dublin.

Pagination: pp. *i-iv, 1,* 2-51, *52* = 56 Pages.

Collation Formula: Crown 8vo.   [A]² B-D⁸ E² = 28 Leaves.

Description: p. *i* title; p. *ii:* Copyright 1918. J. Bernard McCarthy | [Printers Imprint]; p. *iii* dedication: TO MY MOTHER | THIS PLAY IS LOVINGLY

48

DEDICATED; p. *iv*: *DRAMATIS PERSONÆ*; pp. *1*, 2-51 text; p. *52* date of first performance, January 17th, 1917, plus cast.

Paper: Thin very inferior grey wove paper (Newsprint).

Binding: Mid lake wrappers, overlapping all edges, all edges trimmed.

Front Wrapper: Printed black, [across upper portion] CRUSADERS | BERNARD McCARTHY | [line block of a boy holding a theatrical mask in each hand, across top of block: MAUNSEL'S and] across base of block: IRISH PLAYS. Size: 8·9 × 5 cms.] [beneath] ABBEY THEATRE SERIES | One Shilling Net.

Back Wrapper: Printed black, advertisements for books by Padraic Pearse; James Connolly; " A.E."

Inside Front Wrapper: Printed black, advertisements for books by Darrell Figgis.

Inside Back Wrapper: Printed black, advertisements for books about The Rebellion; Books by Alice Stopford Green; Books in Irish.

Format: Crown 8vo.   *Size:* 18·5 × 12 **cms.**

Copies Examined: F.-J.F., L.M., N.L.I., B.M., Bod., U.L.C., A.L.E., J.O'L., U.C.D.

Published, *English Catalogue,* July, 1918; N.L.I. Stamp, 3 JUL 1918; B.M. Stamp, 30 AUG 18; Bod. Stamp, 24 OCT 1919; U.L.C. Stamp, OC 20 1919; A.L.E. Stamp, 20 OCT 1919; price, 1/-.

Notes: Crusaders is still in print.

24

ABBEY THEATRE SERIES (Second Series), Vol. 9.

Maurice Dalton, *Sable and Gold*, Maunsel and Roberts, Ltd., Dublin. January, 1922.

SABLE AND GOLD | A PLAY IN THREE ACTS | BY MAURICE DALTON | MAUNSEL AND ROBERTS LTD.

Printers Imprint: p. *iv* [at foot of page] Printed by Maunsel & Roberts Ltd., Dublin.

Pagination: pp. *i-viii, 1*, 2-55, *56* = 64 **Pages.**

Collation Formula: [A]⁴ B-C⁸ D⁴ E⁸ = 32 Leaves.

Description: pp. *i-ii* blank; p. *iii* title; p. *iv* Printers Imprint; pp. *v-vi:* PREFACE [signed] MAURICE DALTON; p. *vii: DRAMATIS PERSONÆ* [plus] Scene; pp. *1*, 2-55 text; p. *56* Place and date of first performance—

Father Matthew Hall, Cork, 15 May, 1918, plus cast.

Paper: Antique cream wove paper.

Binding: Bronze green wrappers, overlapping all edges, all edges trimmed.

Front Wrapper: Printed black, [across upper portion] SABLE AND GOLD |
A PLAY IN THREE ACTS | BY MAURICE DALTON | [line block of a
boy holding a theatrical mask in each hand, across top of block: MAUNSEL'S
[and] across base of block: IRISH PLAYS. Size: 8·9 × 5 cms.] | [beneath]
ABBEY THEATRE SERIES | Two Shillings Net.

Inside Front Wrapper: Printed black, [across centre] *Rights of Performances
Reserved.*

Format: Crown 8vo.   *Size:* 18·3 × 12·4 cms.

Copies Examined: F.-J.F., T.C.D., L.M., B.M., Bod., U.L.C., A.L.E.

Published, *English Catalogue,* January, 1922; T.C.D. Stamp, 19 JAN 1922;
B.M. Stamp, 20 JAN 1922; Bod. Stamp, JUL 1922; U.L.C. Stamp, JY 20 1922;
A.L.E. Stamp, 24 JUL 1922; price, 2/-.

Notes: Sable and Gold was first produced by the Abbey Theatre Co. on 16th
September, 1918.

Sable and Gold is still in print.

APPENDIX

SCHEMA OF IMPRESSIONS AND ISSUES

FIRST SERIES

Schema of Impressions and Issues

Volumes	I	II	III	IV	V	VI	VII	VIII	IX	X	XI	XII	XIII	XIV	XV
	1 A Ia February 1905	2 A ?April 1905	3 A ? 1905	4 ? 1905	5 ? 1905	6 ?December 1905	7 A ? 1905	8 ? 1906	9 A ?September 1906	10 A ?February 1907	11 February 1908	12 November 1909	13 A I ?May 1910	14 A I April 1911	15 June 1911
	1 A Ib ?February 1905														
	1 A II ? 1905														
													13 A II ?October 1911	14 A II ?April 1911	
		2 B ? 1906	3 B ? 1905				7 B ? 1906		9 B December 1907	10 B ?November 1909				14 B ? 1912	
														14 C I ?	
														14 C II ?	

KEY

Arabic Numerals	= Volumes.
Capital Letters	= Impressions.
Roman Numerals	= Issues.
Lower Case Letters	= Simultaneons Issues.

SECOND SERIES

Schema of Impressions and Issues

Volumes	1	2	3	4	5	6	7	8	9
	16 October 1911	17 A Ia June 1912	18 A Ia June 1912	19 A Ia June 1912	20 A Ia February 1914	21 A Ia April 1914	22 A June 1917	23 July 1918	24 January 1922
		17 A Ib June 1912	18 A Ib June 1912	19 A Ib June 1912	20 A Ib February 1914	21 A Ib April 1914			
		17 A II ?		19 A II ?November 1912					
		17 B ?							

21 B I ?	22 B ?September 1919
21 B II ?	
	22 C ?

KEY

Arabic Numerals	= Volumes.
Capital Letters	= Impressions.
Roman Numerals	= Issues.
Lower Case Letters	= Simultaneous Issues.